Also by Terry McDermott

The Hunt for KSM: Inside the Pursuit and Takedown of the
Real 9/11 Mastermind, Khalid Sheikh Mohammed

101 Theory Drive: The Discovery of Memory

Perfect Soldiers: The 9/11 Hijackers—Who They Were,
Why They Did It

OFF SPEED

OFF SPEED

*Baseball, Pitching,
and the Art of Deception*

TERRY McDERMOTT

Pantheon Books, New York

Grateful acknowledgment is made to W. W. Norton & Company, Inc.
for permission to reprint an excerpt of "Iowa Déjà Vu" from *Making
Certain It Goes On: Collected Poems of Richard Hugo* by Richard Hugo.
Copyright © 1984 by The Estate of Richard Hugo. Reprinted by
permission of W. W. Norton & Company, Inc.

The pitching diagrams that appear in this book are reprinted by
permission of Lokesh Dhakar.

Library of Congress Cataloging-in-Publication Data
Name: McDermott, Terry, author.
Title: Off speed : baseball, pitching, and the art of deception /
Terry McDermott.
Description: New York : Pantheon, 2017.
Identifiers: LCCN 2016035366 (print). LCCN 2016051448 (ebook).
ISBN 9780307379429 (hardcover). ISBN 9780307908896 (ebook).
Subjects: LCSH: Pitching (Baseball). Baseball. BISAC: SPORTS &
RECREATION/Coaching/Baseball. SPORTS & RECREATION/
History. SPORTS & RECREATION/Baseball/History.
Classification: LCC GV871.M42 2017 (print). LCC GV871 (ebook).
DDC 796.357/22—dc23
LC record available at lccn.loc.gov/2016035366

www.pantheonbooks.com

Jacket photograph by Tim Clayton / Corbis / Getty Images
Jacket design by Oliver Munday
Book design by M. Kristen Bearse

Printed in the United States of America
First Edition
2 4 6 8 9 7 5 3 1

For Casey, Cary, and Lina,
in partial repayment for what my father gave me

West of here love is opportune.
I get this from the soft cry of a train;
from magazines the barber lets me take.
West, it cools at night. Stars reproduce
like insects and wild horses sing.

—Richard Hugo, "Iowa Déjà Vu"

Don't pitch the cookies.

—Hisashi Iwakuma

CONTENTS

GLOSSARY OF PITCH TYPES

FOUR-SEAM FASTBALL: A straight fastball, almost always the fastest pitch any pitcher can throw. It is called a four-seam fastball because it is gripped across the seams. This is the most common pitch. Speeds can range from low-80s mph to more than 100 mph.

TWO-SEAM FASTBALL: A fastball gripped with the seams rather than across them. The two-seamer sinks and often moves left to right from a right-handed pitcher.

CURVEBALL: The most basic breaking pitch, it is gripped with the middle finger along a seam and thrown with a strong snap of the wrist to the right for a right-handed pitcher; this imparts spin to the ball, causing it to break both horizontally right-to-left and down.

SLIDER: A faster breaking ball than the curve, but slower than a fastball. It breaks more horizontally and less verti-cally than a normal curve. It is not as fast as a fastball but is faster than the rest of a pitcher's pitches. It is gripped like a two-seam fastball but slightly off center, so that the ball is released off the thumb side of the index finger.

CUT FASTBALL: The cutter lies halfway along a continuum between a fastball and a slider. The grip is almost identical to a four-seam fastball, but the fingers are moved slightly to the right and more pressure is put on the ball with the middle finger. There is no wrist snap. To the hitter, the pitch looks identical to a fastball. It breaks very little, but does so very late.

CHANGEUP: A change-of-pace pitch that is thrown as if it is going to be a fastball but that leaves the hand as much as 10 mph slower. The most common change grip in use today is the circle change, in which the index finger and the thumb are used to form a circle to the side of the ball which is held in the other three fingers. The hand is turned so that the circle is facing the ground as the pitch is released. The combination of the grip and the downward turn of the hand lessens the speed of the pitch and often imparts a slight right-to-left break from a right-handed pitcher.

SINKER: Similar to and sometimes synonymous with the two-seam fastball.

SPLITTER, OR SPLIT-FINGERED FASTBALL: Similar to a sinker but with a much sharper downward break. The ball is gripped with the index and middle fingers spread as far as feasible on the outside of the seams. The pitch is thrown with the same motion as a fastball but is typically somewhat slower, and it dives as it reaches the plate.

FORKBALL: Similar to the split-fingered fastball but gripped more deeply in the hand and with somewhat less spread between the top fingers; it is slower and has less spin than the split.

KNUCKLEBALL: An unpredictable, erratic, impossible-to-hit pitch that has little to no spin; it is the only sort of pitch that might break twice in opposite directions. It is gripped not with the knuckles but with the fingertips of the middle and index fingers, placed directly behind the seam. The thumb and ring fingers are placed on opposite sides, also outside the seam. The goal of the pitch is to have as little spin as possible, causing the ball to move unpredictably even when a hitter knows with 100 percent certainty that the knuckler is coming.

EEPHUS: A lob; it has the trajectory of a slow pitch softball pitch. Only one or two pitchers per generation ever throw it in a game.

SCREWBALL: A backward curveball. That is, it breaks down, but in the opposite direction of a curveball. It is gripped like a curve, but the wrist is turned in the opposite direction, toward the pitcher's glove side, upon release.

SPITTER: An illegal pitch to which a foreign substance—saliva, Vaseline, hair cream, or who knows what—has been applied, causing the pitch to drop suddenly as it approaches home plate. It is thrown with the same grip and motion as a fastball. Its trajectory is similar to that of a split-fingered fastball. There is widespread suspicion that many of the great split-finger practitioners were, in fact, throwing spitters, not splits.

PREFACE

If you noted the Richard Hugo stanza on the epigraph page, you might have already guessed what I am about to tell you. Hugo, as regular a guy as has ever made a living writing poetry, wrote often about ordinariness and dreams of escaping it. He never wrote much about baseball, or sport of any kind other than fishing, but at its best, baseball offers what Hugo's verses suggest—a fantasy of beauty rising not above but out of the ordinary. The game would make mysteries of the mundane. It is this quality of baseball that I cherish above all others. Well, that and, as economically expressed by Hisashi Iwakuma, its utter opposite—craft.

We have dressed the game in so many fine coats of so many glorious colors that it becomes hard to see the thing itself. I've occasionally applied some of these coats myself, relishing the myths and sometimes realities of baseball's lovely, stubbornly American past.

I grew up fifteen minutes from the cornfield where they would later build the diamond for that Kevin Costner *Field of Dreams* movie. The film tried hard to ruin a charming little book, and you might consider this project my revenge, but there was an essential truth on display in the book that even Hollywood could not foil. The game's bucolic fantasies seem not at all far-fetched in the patch-work farmland of eastern Iowa. When you walk through those woods, hollows, and fields, you think: Maybe this could have happened. There are real baseball fields in real farm pastures all over the place. Ghosts in the corn, too.

But here's the other side of that: These pastoral fantasies aside, the game can be grim. It can be harsh. Its contes-tants can be as low-minded and mean as any humans on the planet. Hidden among its charms and misty memo-ries lurk diamond-grade shards that will rip you apart. An individual baseball game can look—and be—ungainly. Consider the Seattle Mariners at the Los Angeles Angels of Anaheim, Memorial Day weekend, 2010. My team, the Mariners, came to town with what seem in retrospect comical ambitions. A surprisingly not terrible opening two months of the season had raised the possibility of rel-evance for a downtrodden franchise that had racked up ninety-plus losses a year for most of its existence and had ground through field managers and players at a pace so quick they could be measured by a dot-com burn rate. I could name players you've never heard of for hours. There are hundreds lost in the mist, but who on this earth wants to remember the Mariner tenures of Ben Davis, Bobby Ayala,* or Danny Tartabull?

---

*To avenge but one of the guilty parties, here's all you need to know about Ayala, a relief pitcher on some unexpectedly good Mariner clubs of the mid-1990s. In those days, I was working at a newspaper in Seattle and used to keep track of the scores of the games as they progressed while I worked. I was thus following the course of one late-season game that the Mariners needed to win to stay relevant in a pennant race that was rapidly heading for conclusion. The M's had a three- or four-run lead in the middle innings, and the game seemed

Angel Stadium—the Big A—is a nice enough place for a ball game. This despite the cloying mass of faux rock, installed as part of a "water feature" by a former Disney ownership, beyond the left-center-field fence, and the ever-preening presence of Mike Scioscia, the Angels' manager, installed apparently by God in the home dugout.

Z, a fellow Mariner sufferer, had flown down from Seattle for the weekend series, which had opened nicely the prior evening with an easy M's win. It's eighty degrees; a faint breeze reaches inland Orange County from the Pacific; there is glorious sunshine, good companionship, and better-than-average beer. What could possibly go wrong?

On this glorious sun-kissed afternoon, the full-house crowd's buzz wove through an old friend's conversation, building, like a swarm of bees approaching. If this had been a movie, underneath the gentle hummm we'd have had a full orchestra of Hans Zimmer violins shrieking: Danger ahead. I didn't hear it. Never saw the rough beast approaching. Instead, we had lucked into a tight pitcher's duel between the teams' two aces—Felix Hernandez for Seattle and Jered Weaver for Anaheim. The M's scored an early run off an error, but Weaver, the surfer dude who abides if ever there was one, remained otherwise unhittable, and Hernandez, nicknamed the King when he was still a minor leaguer, was regal and even tougher. When Weaver beat you, you felt like you'd been tricked. When

---

in the bag. But when I saw the final score, they had lost. I called home and asked my daughter what had happened. Cary was, like me, a fan, but, being younger and smarter, hadn't yet fallen for the bullshit. She didn't sugar-coat her answer: Ayala happened, she said. I understood exactly what she meant.

Hernandez did it, you felt like you'd been punished for your inferior genes. As a Mariner fan, I felt that the fact that Weaver beat us more than we beat him was grossly unfair.

The game rolled into the eighth inning with the Mariners' 1–0 lead still standing. Hernandez then grooved a fastball that Bobby Abreu hit out of the park to dead center field, tying the game. Nobody scored in the ninth, and it was on to extras.

The Mariner bullpen had been strong over the past weeks, and we settled in for who knew how long. Then, in the way that baseball can, the easy conversation, the laughter, and the prospect of sunny recollection vanished with the sudden sadness of a left fielder plowing into a wall head-on. The Angels loaded the bases against the M's reliever Brandon League, then Kendrys Morales unloaded on a fastball and, bam, hearts broken at 100.6 mph, the speed at which the ball left the bat en route to the left-center-field papier-mâché rocks. I know about the heartbreak because I was there. I know the speed of the batted ball because of the constant access the Internet provides to almost every measurable data point in every contemporary game. You can now almost instantly know more about every pitch thrown in a big league baseball game than the pitcher who threw it. You can certainly know more about every pitch than somebody watching a game in 1975 knew about any pitch. A sophisticated camera-computer system has been installed in every Major League Baseball park, and it tracks every pitch's approach to the plate by its speed, spin, and angle. Just a decade ago, this was barely imaginable. Now it's routine, and the river of data the technology has unleashed has flooded through the game.

Baseball can turn a fan's world from the movie-sky light of golden California to deep, bleak, satanic rain-forest gloom in the time it takes—as it happens, about three seconds—for a ball to leave a bat and land in the bottom of the tenth inning with a heart-wrenching thud.

I should have seen this coming. The Mariners, raising themselves, we thought, as actual contenders, instead were swept in the last three games of the series. More than swept, they were humiliated and sent tumbling back to their rightful place at the bottom of the standings. It was the way they lost that did the real harm. They lost two of the games in the bottom of the last inning, having led going into it; the other they mercifully kicked away in the eighth. Not even the victors enjoyed it. The Angels' best hitter, Morales, broke his ankle jumping on home plate in celebration of his grand slam. It was season-ending, too. He was gone for the next year and a half. Nobody knew that then, of course. But as he lay there writhing on the ground, nobody was happy, least of all, the Mariner fans in attendance. Like me and Z. We sat there, too old, with too much mileage, and too accustomed to this result to cry. Already damaged goods, we trudged to the exit further impaired for sure. Except for followers of the Chicago Cubs, whose fans have no excuse and less hope, this willing acceptance of pain painted over geologic layers of scars is the price paid for being a fan of a longtime losing sports team.

Morales doesn't know me. Or even of me or all the suspect things I've done in my life. He couldn't possibly have known about the bubble gum playing cards I habitually shoplifted from Oeschger's Grocery. He wasn't even born yet. And he's from Cuba, a very long way from Oeschger's. It's not like he singled me out; the punishment was not in any way personal. So, in examining a crime against nature such as this, you're immediately confronted with the grim observation that there is no motive.

What we have instead are facts. This being baseball, we have lots of them. Foremost, we have League, the Mariner reliever who gave up the long ball. League is a pitcher with a great arm, two great pitches, and apparently no brain. That year, he had one of the best fastballs in the American League, consistently throwing between 95 and 100 mph. It wasn't straight, either. He normally had a great sinking action on the pitch. He also had an unhittable split-fingered pitch that looked exactly like the fastball until it dived straight to earth as it reached the hitter. The problem was that League threw the regular fastball with mechanical regularity, relying on his speed to beat hitters, and reserving the split-finger for situations when he could get a strikeout with it. Meaning, if you were a hitter, you knew pretty much without question what pitch League would throw you to start the at bat—fastball. His was an above-average fastball in both speed and movement, but it was a fastball nonetheless. It is a truism that major league hitters can hit any fastball, no matter the speed, if they know it's coming. As James Shields, a veteran MLB pitcher, put it: "When a major league hitter gets what he's looking for, it's all aboard for a ride to the moon."[1]

Morales knew what was coming. He went to the moon.

. . .

This book began that afternoon with League's mulish obstinacy. Why on earth would a big league pitcher ever give big league hitters the sort of advantage born of utter predictability? Just as I can know the escape velocity of a home run, every team, every hitter, every coach can know with absolute certainty the way opposing pitchers pitch. Gone are the days when hitters and pitchers relied on hand-scratched notepads or folk wisdom for scouting reports. Today they are handed a ream of computer printouts describing every pitch sequence the pitcher has ever thrown. They can receive an iPad with a list of all the at bats they ever had against that day's pitcher, parsed by inning, by count, by barometric pressure if they want it. The pitcher can be given pictorial heat maps showing what pitches on what counts in what sequence work for this hitter and that. He can look at a video montage that shows every 2-1 count a guy has faced for a year.

I can think of but two possible reasons a pitcher might do what League does—stupidity and pride. League is not Einstein, but he isn't a complete oaf, either. He has great hair, really great tattoos, and a lovely family. He's well spoken, seems like a good guy. He's not an inert object on the interview couch, but a somewhat goofy modern athlete. If he's not stupid, we're left with pride. This is often portrayed as self-confidence. Pitchers and catchers say in defense of a pitch selection that went awry that they chose the ill-fated pitch because it was the pitcher's best pitch. "I'm not going to get beat with my second or third pitch," they'll say. Throw the best thing you got. And, they never add, get beat by that.

It is, the Hall of Famer Warren Spahn famously said, the job of the pitcher to fool the hitter. Baseball is a game of timing, he said. The pitcher's job is to upset the hitter's timing. This is done in one of two ways. The ball is thrown in such a way that it arrives in the vicinity of home plate in a manner the hitter does not expect. The ball is not where it is supposed to be in either time or space. That is, you're looking for a fastball, and it's not. Because it's something slower, it arrives at the plate fractions of a second too late. It's not where your brain told you it was going to be. Or its trajectory was somehow altered, and not always in obvious ways. The ball has moved because of gravity, wind, magic, or deceit.

That is what this book is about: how pitchers fool, or try to fool, hitters, and how this has evolved for more than a century. I have tried to sample both the wealth of anecdotal evidence on the subject and the vast array of data that has only in recent years become available. The book follows in some detail the course of a single game. That game, of course, involves my Seattle Mariners. How could it not? The game, Felix Hernandez's perfect game in 2012, is one of the greatest exhibitions of off-speed pitches ever put on. There have been more than two hundred thousand games played over the past century-plus of Major League Baseball history. There have been just twenty-three perfect games among them. No one epitomized the wonder of baffling hitters more than did Hernandez that day. This book gives a detailed account of the game and diverges from it at various points throughout to provide relevant historic, scientific, or discursive information.

I've tried to incorporate, too, a sampling of the sort of statistical analysis that is revolutionizing the contemporary game. Anyone reading this book will already be aware of the battle that has gone on within baseball between traditionalists and the now not-so-new wave of statistical analysts. It is beyond irony that a sport well known for scrupulously gathering, compiling, even honoring its data has become embroiled in a loud dispute about the value of data. For convenience, we will refer to the two opposing camps as the traditionalists and the sabermetricians, named for their organization, the Society for American Baseball Research. The dispute between the two groups is mainly about which data are important.

Traditional and sabermetric analyses differ mainly in focus. Traditionalists tend to look at results—what happened? Sabermetricians look at process—why? This leads the two sides to value different units of measurement. Sabermetrics regards the base unit of the game as the out. There are twenty-seven of them on each side of the ball. Spend them wisely on offense; maximize their creation on defense. Traditional baseball analysis is concerned mostly with runs—how many did you score and how many did you allow. Many of the traditional metrics—runs allowed, runs scored, runs driven in—measure runs directly. Most of the friction between traditional analysts and sabermetricians derives from these basic orientations. Given the nature of baseball and the aforementioned amount of romance with which it historically has been engaged, there is an almost built-in antagonism between the two groups.

I've been a fan of baseball most of my life. I knew it initially as a totally inept player. My first Little League season, I bunted and prayed for walks. It didn't work. I went 0 for the entirety of 1956. I loved playing; I just wasn't any good. We played at every opportunity. We played pickup games when we could come up with enough players, wiffle-ball games when we couldn't come up with a real ball. We hit fly balls and grounders to one another until the cows came home. We threw balls off of walls and pitched into nets, providing play-by-play analysis with every throw. I played baseball board games and played games on the living room floor in which the ball was a crumpled piece of newsprint and the bat was a playing card.

At the same time, I devoured big league box scores. My dad was a Yankee fan, and so therefore was I. I charted their progress through the daily reports in the Dubuque *Telegraph Herald* and the compilation of league averages in the Sunday *Des Moines Register*. Like Richard Hugo, the poet quoted in the epigraph to this book, I savored the first magazines I found. Mine were in Jake's Barber Shop in downtown Cascade, Iowa. Copies of *The Sporting News* lay there. What an astonishing discovery that was. An entire magazine devoted to nothing but baseball, containing every statistic I could imagine. This was heaven, a country I was to discover, encompassing a far larger and richer expanse than I knew. I read my way through every baseball biography and John Tunis novel the Dubuque County Library bookmobile contained. I wanted more, even though by then my head was stuffed with more romantic bullshit than any head could possibly hold. It didn't explode, but on more than one occasion came very close.

My father was a reader, too, but tended toward more useful subjects—history, war, Mickey Spillane. He hadn't much use for sloth, at least not as practiced by me. He seemed okay with an occasional indulgence for himself. He regularly sprawled on the living room floor for a mid-day nap. He would have a couple of lazy beers on a Sunday afternoon, lying in the shade with a radio playing whatever game we could fetch from the airwaves. By and large, though, he was industrious and responsible, and he was right about me. I was a sloth. Unlike him, I wondered how I would ever get anywhere. With one notable exception,* he was largely content to remain in Cascade. He went off to war and came back and settled in. He had seen enough of the world to know where he wanted to be. I knew early on that the one place I wanted be was anywhere else. For most of its mile-long length, Cascade was just a couple blocks wide. You could look down almost any side street and see cornfields and pastures. It felt to me like I was as easy to see through as the town and there were entirely too many people who wanted a peek.

Then, one day in seventh grade, I had a revelation. We had been assigned an in-class essay on Africa. Being the sort of student who never did any of the required work, I realized that, other than its location, I knew nothing about Africa. I'm almost certain I couldn't have named five countries. South Africa, I thought probably. Egypt? Is that in Africa? Who knows. Dark continent indeed—to

*To be more fully explained later.

me it was a black hole. Fortunately, however, I was sitting directly behind Monica Hosch, Veronica's twin. The two were among the smartest kids in class, and Monica was rapidly filling up the first of what I assumed would be many pages of African insight. I couldn't see what she was writing other than the title she had given it—something about Africa's inevitable booming development.

Desperate, I stole her idea and whipped out a thousand words on the shining African moment about to arrive. Of course it was pure fantasy, but I had at least avoided turning in a blank sheet of paper. Imagine my shock when the teacher returned the graded papers and she had given me an A with rousing praise in her comments. Turned out, I guess, I had a skill, enhanced somewhat by the fact that Sister Mary Ana Martine apparently knew as much about Africa as I did, but a skill nonetheless.

I regarded this as a sign and took my first step to becoming a writer that day. Thanks to Sister Mary Ana Martine and Monica, I've spent most of my adult life reporting and writing. I like to think I've been regarded as a serious, diligent, fact-obsessed journalist. Still, this is a book about baseball. So what you have is a combination of serious reporting and baseball's considerable store of its own myths. Somewhere in here I hope they intersect in a way not unlike the path of an effortless outfielder meeting an arcing line drive in the deep-right-center-field gap—in a way, in other words, that might bring a smile to the most hardened of baseball hearts.

OFF SPEED

THE FASTBALL

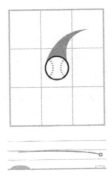

It is a typically gorgeous, sunny Wednesday afternoon in Seattle. To outlanders, the sun might seem a surprise, but Seattle summers are drenched in sunshine and dry, with long, languid evenings that can outlast a night game. If this is at odds with the image of Seattle as a wet, dark, and dour place inhabited mainly by caffeine addicts, hikers, and perhaps hobbits, well, it's only a seasonal departure. It rains every day from November through June. A constant cloak of low gray clouds hangs like a mighty weight pressing down on your disposition. If the sun rises and sets—as has been rumored—it does so in secret, unseen by mortal men and women.

But once summer actually starts—stow the calendar, this is typically some days, perhaps weeks, after the Fourth of July—Seattle is a very summery place. This afternoon's getaway game features the visiting Tampa Bay Rays versus the home-standing Seattle Mariners. The teams are headed in opposite directions—the Rays streaking up into the thick, dangerous atmosphere of a pennant race, the Mariners stumbling down the basement staircase. Again.

The Mariners don't have enough history to have become endearing like the Cubs or bitterly tragic like the once and possibly future Red Sox. They lack the brickworked ivy or sentimental melodramatics necessary to usher the franchise into cultural sainthood. There is abundant misery here, but few martyrs. The team has nonetheless been very good at losing. They've played thirty-nine seasons and have finished with more wins than losses in about a third of them. They made it to the playoffs in four of those winning seasons, slightly more than once per decade. They are at this writing one of only two current franchises that have never played in the World Series, much less won it.*

The 2012 season, like so many before it, had become a lost cause well before the All-Star break. Yet another rebuilding plan was under way, and the lineup had been

---

*You can see in this qualification—"at this writing"—the far-gone quality of being a fan, suggesting as it does that somehow between the time this is written and the time you read it, the Mariners might actually appear in a World Series. I can't help myself.

turned over to prospects and pretenders in the hope of finding out which were which. The team's lone star, Ichiro Suzuki, recently had been traded off to enemy lands to give him a last chance at glory and, not inconveniently, remove his huge salary from future payrolls. Unusually for such a wretched team, Seattle had produced a number of the game's great players over the past quarter-century— the exquisite artist Ichiro; the sluggers Ken Griffey, Jr., and Alex Rodriguez; the best right-handed hitter of his generation, Edgar Martinez; and one of the most intimidating pitchers of all time, the gangly, angry southpaw Randy Johnson.

Ichiro was—oddly, given some of the things he did in the batter's box—supremely elegant and a big fan favorite. He has also been one of the best players in the majors for a decade and is the last link to any past greatness the franchise had ever enjoyed—he was the American League's Most Valuable Player in 2001, when the team won a major league record of 116 games.

The man who is supposed to be the foundation upon which future greatness would be built, Felix Hernandez, is taking the mound this Wednesday afternoon. Hernandez, a husky right-hander, had been a genuine, classically old-fashioned teen-age phenom, arriving for good in the major leagues as a nineteen-year-old flamethrower in 2005. He had been signed by the Mariners as a pudgy sixteen-year-old high school kid from Valencia, Venezuela. His abilities were so advanced he was given the blogosphere nickname King Felix almost as soon as he started his brief three-year minor league apprenticeship. He had since lived up to the name, quickly becoming one of the best pitchers in the game. Winning the American League's Cy Young award in 2010 merely formalized his status.

Despite his team's lousy record, Hernandez was having one of his better seasons in 2012. In the weeks before this game, he had been virtually unhittable. Included in that stretch were complete game shutouts against the entrenched powers of the league—the Texas Rangers, New York Yankees, and Boston Red Sox. In eleven starts, he had given up on average a hit every other inning and had allowed more than two runs just once. His earned run average over that span was 1.73. He was striking out five times as many people as he walked.

Opposing hitters were reduced to mumbles. David Ortiz, the great Red Sox slugger, suggested King Felix was inhuman. Ortiz's teammate Dustin Pedroia said after one game that in four at bats against Hernandez, he was thrown just a single pitch that he thought it was even possible to hit.[1]

Consider the major league hitter's basic problem. The pitcher stands on a small hill sixty feet six inches—give or take a foot, depending on where in the batter's box the hitter stands—away. The pitcher strides forward before he throws, and, by the time he releases the ball, has already shrunk the distance between him and the hitter by almost 10 percent. An average fastball from an average pitcher leaves his hand at about 90 mph. A pitcher of average size throwing at average speed gives the hitter approximately four-tenths of a second to see, identify, and attack a pitch. That is about how long it takes to blink your eyes twice.[2]

The batter is using an implement uniquely unsuitable

to accomplishing his task. A baseball bat is normally some-what less than a yard long; it weighs somewhere between twenty-nine and thirty-six ounces. At its thickest part it is 2.25 inches in diameter. If the bat is to strike the ball solidly, the ball must hit near the center of the bat's cir-cumference about six inches from the bat's end. The spot varies from bat to bat, depending on the type and hard-ness of the wood and the shape and weight of the bat, but at its largest this spot is about five square inches in area.

Think of that for a moment. A hitter must swing a yard-long piece of round wood in such a way that he contacts a small round ball moving faster than he is legally allowed to drive his car. The contact has to occur within a five-square-inch area of the wood. The plane of the strike zone varies from hitter to hitter but is theoretically seventeen inches wide and approximately two feet tall. Of course, the zone is not a plane at all, but a volume of approxi-mately 4.5 cubic feet. It extends from the front of home plate to the rear, and a ball passing through it at any point is supposed to be a strike.[3] In real life, the zone tends to be wider and shorter than the rulebook stipulates. Nonethe-less, the batter is defending more than four cubic feet of space with a five-square-inch weapon, and he has to swing the bat at a speed of 70 mph in order to move it from his shoulder to the center of the plate. "It is far more likely that the pitcher will accidentally throw the ball in the way of the hitter's bat than it is for the hitter to time the pitch perfectly and execute flawless swing mechanics to achieve 100 percent on-time contact on their own," according to Perry Husband, who has studied pitcher-batter interac-tions extensively.[4]

The deck, in other words, is stacked.* As long as he doesn't throw the ball at the hitter's head, a pitcher can do pretty much anything he wants. And sometimes he can also do that. Baseball is one of the few sports in which the defense—the pitcher's team—initiates the action. The hitter is on offense in name only. The offense is utterly reactive and is only called the offense because the score is kept depending on how it performs. It's as if the middle linebacker scored a point every time he stuffed a run in the three-hole. The nomenclature derives from baseball's earliest days, when the pitcher's sole job was to set the play in motion. In the mid-nineteenth century, pitchers threw underhand and were required not to do anything to deceive the hitter. Runs scored by the dozen. Games lasted all day. Things have changed.

With a few exceptions, some notable,† the history of baseball since has been an arms race, pitchers developing new weapons to deploy against hitters. Every time hitters

---

*This is a bigger problem for some hitters than others. Henry Aaron, one of the great sluggers in the game's history, early in his career with the Milwaukee Braves didn't think the pitcher had much if any advantage. "The pitcher has got only a ball," he said. "I've got a bat. So the percentage of weapons is in my favor and I let the fellow with the ball do the fretting."

† One obvious exception was the steroid era; another was the lowering of the pitcher's mound after Bob Gibson's 1968 season, during which he did a convincing portrayal of what would happen if a deity came to earth and pitched in the National League. He allowed on average two runs a week and set the all-time record for lowest earned run average, 1.12. Every time I type that number, I think it can't possibly be right. It is. Among other far-fetched accomplishments, Gibson completed twenty-eight out of the thirty-four games he started. Thirteen of those games were shutouts. Today, a pitcher who throws three shutouts has a good chance to lead his league. If someone threw thirteen, he would be given a billion dollars and sent to the Hall of Fame forthwith.

somehow manage to catch up, pitchers regroup and devise new weapons.

It began with allowing pitchers to get a running start, as in a cricket match, then throwing overhand; pretty soon pitchers were doing everything they could dream up to frustrate hitters. They smeared mud on the ball, scratched and scarred it, spit on it, threw it from every arm angle they could achieve. The worst of this—well, a little of the worst of this—was gradually eliminated, and by the turn of the twentieth century the game had a regularized set of rules, an established strike zone, and looked more or less like the modern game.[5]

This is not to say that the experience of attending a game is remotely like what it was then. I saw my first professional games in, I think, 1959, a Yankee–White Sox doubleheader at Comiskey. Cascade was a couple hundred miles west of Chicago, and once a year a group of local men would charter a Burlington Line train—who knew you could even do this?—out of East Dubuque, Illinois. They'd fill the train with Knights of Columbus, cold ham sandwiches, and Falstaff beer—or maybe Schlitz in a good year—and head east. My father, known to everyone as Mac, took me along as an early birthday gift.

It was my first game, my first train, my first taxi, my first bus, my first time seeing grown men pass out drunk. That would be the stranger seated next to me at the park, not one of the Cascade men, all of whom knew how to drink very well, thank you.

We left Cascade in the pre-dawn dark in Buck Menster's sunburned Chevy sedan, went to early Mass at the cathedral in Dubuque, then crossed the Mississippi River into Illinois and boarded the train. The men played cards and talked. I'm not sure I said ten words the entire day; my tongue couldn't catch up to my eyes. I stared at the passing countryside through the open doors of the club car, a freight car with a bar of two-by-six planks set upon fifty-five-gallon drums and a couple of iced trash cans.

Once in Chicago and out of the maze that was the Fourteenth Street rail yard, we went for lunch to a downtown cafeteria, where I was allowed for the first time in my life to order whatever I wanted. I chose half a chicken, which we determined back at our table hadn't really been cooked to the expectations of an eight-year-old. My father advised me that in the future I ought to get the roast beef. Can't go wrong with beef, he said: they never undercook it. I filed this under things it was good to know, not realizing that there was an obvious alternative—cook the chicken.

As we ate, I continued staring, now not at farm fields but at the black people around us in the restaurant. They spoke an exotic language I didn't understand. They had coffee-colored palms and bright-white teeth with gold fillings. This was a long way from home.

The games themselves were a blur. We were Yankee fans then, followers of a royal dynasty that ruled over baseball like visiting kings over colonized lands. Even if you had a set to receive it, there wasn't much major league baseball on television then. We followed the sport in print and on the radio. Even radios were hard to come by—not everybody owned one. I built my own out of a crystal set but had to clip it to tall metal objects to get any reception beyond Cedar Rapids. I spent a lot of time sitting on the grass next to St. Martin's Church, my radio attached to the tallest rain pipe in town.

At Comiskey, we waited for the Yankee players to come up through a tunnel to the field, hoping for autographs. I was shocked at how small they were. I had expected giants; instead, they didn't look much different from the men I knew in Cascade, and just as surly, too. Baseball remains the professional game for normal-sized humans, not the beanpoles on basketball courts or the blocks of muscle roving around football fields.

Comiskey was an ancient, crumbling temple. Structural supports obstructed views almost everywhere. You were constantly forced to stick your head into the shoulder or neck of the person next to you to follow the course of a fly ball. I saw the Yankee stars Mickey Mantle, Whitey Ford, and Moose Skowron. The Sox sent out Minnie Minoso, Luis Aparicio,* and Nellie Fox. I had a Nellie Fox bat at home. It was a town-team discard I had put back together with two one-inch wooden screws. Today, with its thick handle and almost complete absence of taper, it might be mistaken for a fence post. Yogi Berra caught both ends of the doubleheader for the Yanks, but let a pop foul fall behind him without even getting to his feet in one of the games. The hitter, Al Smith, I think, predictably homered on the next pitch.

---

*As long as I'm noting lifetime firsts: I'm pretty sure Minoso was the first Cuban and Aparicio the first Venezuelan I ever saw. Or heard of.

On the train home that night, we stood in the open air between cars, a delight and a clear violation of child safety laws. I leaned against the door and stained my shirt—a merit badge for our wild living. Later, inside the car, I pretended to sleep, already preparing the day's events for safekeeping. My father told the man sitting next to us: "I think he had too much for one day." No, Mac, I had exactly enough.

Seattle's Safeco Field is a typical example of the modern baseball stadium. Old parks were fields partially enclosed by rickety bleachers and fences. The new parks are finely hewed factories whose main outputs are pleasure and money. Safeco's design reflects the post–Camden Yards immersion in retro-stadium style—lots of brick and exposed steelwork—but is saved from fashion by a Northwestern plainspokenness. The stadium sits south of downtown Seattle in what had been a light-industrial and warehousing district that primarily served the busy waterfront docks just a couple blocks to the west.* It has a rolling roof that can be closed to counter the rain. The roof moves on steel wheels fed power from giant spools of electric cable that look as if they might have started life in a Harold Lloyd movie. Seattle, for most of its short life,

---

*I thought at the time and still do that the stadium was built in the wrong place, a quarter-mile south of where the Kingdome was, just far enough to make it inconvenient to walk to it from downtown Seattle. Although this had not yet been decided, it seemed clear at the time that the Kingdome was going to be torn down and a new football stadium built in its place, which is precisely what happened. Now the football stadium, which is used a couple dozen times a year, is exactly where the baseball stadium should have been.

has been a gruff, hard place. The stadium captures that and locates the trendy, hipper new city inside and out of sight, where it belongs.

The park avoids some of the most intrusive aspects of contemporary professional sports. There is a lot of quiet on a baseball field, long moments when nothing happens. Much of this used to be filled with chatter—players yipping and yapping encouragement or criticism to one another, mostly to the pitcher and, from the other side, to the hitter. This has largely disappeared, and, surely to prevent crickets from conquering the local soundscape, major league teams fill nearly every empty moment with some sort of synthesized racket. Sometimes this is electronic cheerleading, which, as far as it goes, is fine. Usually, though, the noise is a sort of mindless medley of old rock and roll riffs. Safeco inflicts less of this on its patrons than do many other places.

The park has one of the best beer selections in the big leagues, with lots of comfortable spots to drink it. It has all the now usual amenities—baby-diaper changing rooms, cocktail lounges, vegan burgers—and some Seattle-specific items—Ivar's fried clams and Ichiroll sushi. It has exploding scoreboards and animated speedboat races and more scrolling LED panels than you can possibly read. If you attempted to keep up with all the electronic information, you'd see not a single pitch in the game.

The experience of watching a contemporary major league game here or in any other park is not remotely similar to what one would have found in the 1930s. Or even the eighties.

Safeco was constructed at a cost of half a billion dollars,

most of it from taxpayers. The decision to build the park, and eventually demolish its predecessor, the Kingdome, was made in the months immediately after the 1995 team made an epic late-season run to win their division for the first time ever, then bested the imperious Yankees in a five-game series, the concluding game of which remains the high point of Mariner history. (Given the rest of Mariner history, the game didn't need to rise all that far, but it was nonetheless a spectacular moment.)

The Kingdome had been a truly miserable place to watch, and play, baseball. The building, with its huge cast-concrete beams, was an engineering marvel. From the exterior, it was exceptionally ugly, with a gray, almost Soviet, brutality. Inside, it was a dim, damp cavern, and mostly empty.

The summer after my middle daughter, Cary, was born, I spent many Saturday and Sunday afternoons at the ballpark. I always sat in the left-field bleachers, where you could get as much room as you wanted. Cary slept in a basket on the bench seat beside me. Together we took up four paying spaces. We could have had eight.

Because the crowds were so sparse, it was deathly quiet. Imagine a newborn napping at a contemporary Major League Baseball game. This was another time and place. From where we sat in left field, you could hear fans talking behind first base if their voices rose at all above a conversational volume. I regularly talked with the Mariner left fielder, Phil Bradley. Well, I didn't really talk with Bradley, but *at* him, complaining about what I perceived to be his lack of desire. Bradley was an exceptional athlete—an all-conference quarterback in college—but had what could only be characterized as an insolent physical presence. He slouched. I hated watching him play; he reminded me too much of myself, I guess.*

In part because the Kingdome was so unpleasant, and in larger part because the team was so horrible, the owners of the franchise were always either going broke or threatening to move, often both. The franchise had been plagued from its beginning with bad baseball and low attendance. Sometimes the local citizenry cared; sometimes they didn't. The latest owner to have made the threat seemed the surest to carry it out. Jeff Smulyan, an Indianapolis-based owner of radio stations and small magazines, had purchased the team in 1989 from a miserly southern California real estate developer, George Argyros, who was one of those people who think that because they have succeeded at business, and because the business of America was business, then, of course, they have to be great Americans. Argyros seldom hesitated to let you know this. In fact, he seldom hesitated to let you know anything he was thinking. He was

---

*Years later, I sat in far better seats, behind first base, in beautiful downtown Hiroshima, where the home-standing Fighting Carp were already in trouble in the bottom of the first. The visiting Yomiuri Giants had runners at the corners with one out and the cleanup hitter coming to the plate. The crowd, which had barely had time to slurp a bowl of noodles, was being rallied by a rough-hewn, already drunken cheerleader, who was making it his personal mission to convince me that America had no monopoly on idiocy, when up to the plate slouched—Could it be? Could it not be? Who else ever walked with such studied disdain for his surroundings?—my ol' buddy Bradley. He looked to be his same surly self. In the way these things have gone, I'm sure the Japanese thought him lazy. He is not. He just acts that way. "Bradley, you're still a bum!" I hollered. "Dick Williams wants you!" I shouted, knowing the enmity between Bradley and this past, autocratic Mariner manager. My voice, flat, rude, and foreign, cut through the Japanese night. Bradley, at the plate, shuddered reflexively and spit seeds.

a tough, bulldoggish guy, but straightforward. Smulyan was a much more modern, sophisticated man. He knew the right things to say and said them as he needed. He was handsome and nattily dressed, and always seemed to have just arrived from a sunny vacation.

He promised, as all new sports team owners must, to develop talent and build a base for sustained success, both on and off the field. He seemed a much more Seattle type and was welcomed as a savior. That didn't last long. Smulyan's purchase of the club was highly leveraged; he was overextended financially from the moment he hit town, and unprepared for the sort of operating losses he would encounter.

In order to secure a new loan to cover those losses, he agreed to the bank's requirement that he seek to move the team out of town to a more lucrative market. His plan, he told the bank, was to drive down attendance, allowing him to exercise an escape clause from his lease, then move the team to Florida, where the city of Tampa had a ready stadium but no team.* When the plan was leaked to *The Seattle Times,* an uproar predictably ensued. Smulyan did his best to limit the damage, by acknowledging the veracity of the bank documents but claiming they did not reveal his true aim. Everybody lies to their bankers, he said.[6]

Perhaps, but no one in Seattle seemed willing to determine whom Smulyan was lying to—his bankers or his fans.

---

*It seems hilarious now to consider moving a team to the Tampa dome a threat, but this was before anyone had ever played a game in it, and baseball was expert at extorting tax money to keep franchises where they were.

In what amounted to a fire sale, Smulyan unloaded the club to a group led by Hiroshi Yamauchi, chairman of the Japanese video game company Nintendo, whose American subsidiary was headquartered in a Seattle suburb. The new group included local minority owners, and just two years after purchasing the club, they began complaining that they needed a new ballpark so they could increase revenues in order to cover annual operating losses.*

The '95 team rose from the ruins of that sad history. The team included four of the five greatest Mariners ever—Griffey, Martinez, Johnson, and a teen-aged Rodriguez, so fresh-faced he could have been a Disney star—and surmounted the Dome's imperfections.† They stumbled through the first half of the season but became one of the best teams in baseball after the All-Star break. For the first time in franchise history, the team was a subject of conversation all over town. Soccer moms and dads, huddled over their steaming Starbucks take-away cups, relived and reveled over every improbable comeback all over the city throughout the early autumn. When the team barely squeaked into the playoffs, people stopped traffic to stand in the middle of the street and discuss the events. Drivers didn't honk; they rolled down windows and joined the conversation.

---

* Since the construction of Baltimore's Camden Yards, new, more fan-friendly stadia typically have been greeted by increases in attendance, with accompanying increases in ticket sales and stadium concession sales. Stadium revenues have once again become a substantial factor in team finances, helping to give franchise owners leverage in demanding local financing for new ballparks.

† By this point, the Dome was literally falling apart. Huge sections of insulation sprayed on the underside of the concrete roof had begun falling onto the field, necessitating a monthlong road trip by the team.

Fans packed the Dome for a series against the evil New York Yankees, so much so that tickets were hard to come by, and the dismal dump of a ballpark, packed to its soot-gray roof by deliriously unhinged locals, actually became a genuine home-field advantage for the M's. The Mariners dropped the first two games in the series in New York but once back home in the ugly confines stormed back to tie the series. The New Yorkers couldn't get Griffey and Martinez out. There were several years when nobody could.

In the fifth and final game, we couldn't obtain enough tickets in one place to have the family sit together. Cary, the baby sleeping on the bench seat, was by then almost nine years old and tearing up Little League, with a batting stance that looked frighteningly Edgarian. She was a veteran of scores, if not hundreds, of games, so, when the only ticket we could scrounge was a single in the right-field bleachers, she was perfectly content to spend the evening among strangers. She had a great seat in the front row, surrounded by a bunch of construction workers from across Elliott Bay in Bremerton. This was not the most genteel group to sit your child among—who knows what evil lies in the hearts of Bremertonians, not to mention construction workers—but I had to work, and Millie, her mother, was sitting with friends in far worse seats up among the concrete roof beams.

I sneaked into the press box. From there, I kept an eye on Cary throughout the game with binoculars. By the fourth inning, she and the Bremerton crew were old friends. They bought her souvenirs; I never did. I'm sure by the seventh she was contemplating adoption. At the game's climactic moment, in the eleventh inning—with little Joey Cora and the great Griffey scoring the tying and winning runs on Edgar's line double (known in local lore as The Double) into the left-field corner—the place went berserk. After watching Griffey slide safely into home, I lifted the binoculars to right field to see the burly Bremerton boys high-fiving little Cary.*

The Double, in a very real way, saved baseball in Seattle. The team had been threatening to leave for most of its existence, and the win over the Yankees created just enough popular support to pay for the new stadium, named for a local insurance company, Safeco.

WARMING UP

Other than the obvious—Is Mariano Rivera an alien? Where does Tony La Russa get his hair done? How long will it take this time for Jeffrey Loria to demolish another Marlins team?—there are few mysteries in contemporary baseball. The game is studied and scouted to a degree that would make Boeing engineers envious. If there is a correlation yet uncovered, it's apt to be the equivalent of a species of six-toed sloth in the Laotian highlands—it might exist, but is so rare no one has ever seen it.

Every action, or, in the case of managerial decisions,

---

* Cary turned out to be tougher than anyone could have imagined. She inherited my disdain for authority of all sorts and did not hide it. She was booted from her high school softball team for what the coach insisted was attempted murder. She had thrown a ball from some distance behind him that thrillingly teased the hair coming out from under his cap. He claimed she was trying to kill him. Cary's response was, um, indignant. "If I wanted to hit him," she said, "I would have."

inaction, has two separate incarnations—the brief point in time when it actually occurs and its digital afterlife, which might well be eternal. As the SABR revolution has sniped its way through baseball analysis, picking off one sacred cow after another—they were easy to hit, unexamined assumptions just sitting there in the middle of the field—the afterlife portion of any one baseball event has grown a million-fold.

Legions of fans, sleuths, and statisticians have pored through thousands of old newspapers and reconstructed the game's statistical history from the ground up. As abetted by computers and sophisticated video equipment, nearly everything that happens on a baseball field today is instantly transported into the digital realm. Some of these events have been recorded long before Bill James coined the term "SABR." Certain pitchers kept a book on every hitter. Some kept a book on every pitch. Teams charted their own and opposing pitchers. Managers like Earl Weaver kept binders of hitter-pitcher matchups. Even the most unsophisticated observers knew some of this stuff: that most hitters performed better against opposite-handed pitchers, for example. Hitting platoons—players being switched in and out of the lineup to gain handedness advantage—were actually more prevalent decades ago than they are now.*

---

*This is mainly because team rosters have been set at a maximum of twenty-five active players for most of the last century, and the number of those twenty-five who are pitchers has steadily expanded as bullpen usage has become more specialized. Teams used to carry ten pitchers and fifteen position players. Most teams now have twelve, sometimes thirteen pitchers on their rosters. In effect, teams now platoon their pitchers instead of their hitters.

The smartest franchises incorporated this information into their operations much more quickly than others,* but by now every team has what are called analytics or "baseball information" departments.† The data collected and created by these statisticians are made available to the coaching staff and players. Pitchers or hitters could call up video of every time they faced their opposite numbers with a 2-1 count at night in August on the road. Or any count in any month. You can know how your opponent acts and reacts in virtually every circumstance. You can—literally; you can do this at home—generate graphic depictions of how well every hitter performs on every count against every type of pitch thrown to every sector of the strike zone. Retired players, who, if they were lucky, might be able to watch an opponent once in a great while on television, look at this and are amazed at what they might have done had they possessed such information.

It balances out, however. For every datum a hitter has access to, the pitcher has its mirror image. What does he swing at on what count to what side of the plate at what speed?

Typically, coaches—pitching coaches for pitchers and catchers, hitting coaches for hitters—meet with players before the start of every series to discuss which of their opponent's players has been doing what lately. They also meet before each game with that day's relevant players.

---

*The Texas Rangers are believed to have been the first franchise to have hired a sabermetrician, Craig Wright.
†What other kind of information would a baseball team assemble?

By and large, many contemporary players ignore much of what they're told.

Hernandez is one of those. He almost never watches video of opponents. He might—if something has gone awry—watch video of himself. "Everyone's different," said Carl Willis, Hernandez's pitching coach at the time. "There are some pitchers watch a tremendous amount of video. There are others that won't watch that much. They just trust their feel and their ability. . . . It comes down to are you going to attack this guy's weakness, or are you going to pitch to your strengths? And when do you know to go the other way? He has the ability, because he has four above-average pitches—he may tell you five, but they blend together a little bit at times—but he can throw any pitch at any time, regardless of situation, regardless of count. He has that kind of confidence in his own ability, so his game is almost feel. . . . With his ability, then, to change speeds, he really keeps the hitter off balance. When you combine this with—not the fastball he had five, six years ago, but it's still a ninety-two, ninety-four-miles-per-hour fastball. It's not just a little dog. It's really difficult. And so much about the fastball, it's not a hundred percent velocity as much as it is command and movement. And he has all three of those."[7]

The variability of approach is also true of catchers. Some study their opponents relentlessly. Hernandez's catcher today, John Jaso, thinks this is something done to impress pitchers with your studiousness. In some ways, Jaso typifies an older type of player, those who would work part-time at construction in the off-season. He doesn't actually have another job, but does his own home renovations and drives a truck and a bicycle. Though he's paid fabulously, he receives nothing like the fortunes bestowed upon stars.* He knows he isn't going to rewrite the record books. His main career aspiration is to stay in the big leagues for as long as the ride lasts.

Jaso, as a part-timer, never knows when he's going to play. The Mariner manager, Eric Wedge, is sometimes referred to as Sarge. He's not the touchy-feely type. Jaso didn't know he'd be catching Hernandez today until the lineup was posted: "They don't tell you anything. They don't tell you anything in any aspect of baseball. In spring training, you're getting ready to break camp, and the org knows he's going to go back down to AAA, and they know that two, three weeks in advance, and they don't tell you until the last day. You don't know where to get a hotel, where you should get an apartment, Seattle, Tacoma, wherever their AA is. You don't know anything."[8]

Jaso doesn't reject analysis because he's a grizzled veteran, too bored or experienced to know better. He's a laid-back, hip, modern young athlete. He often wears a hippie-length beard. He has never been a full-time starting catcher in the major leagues. Jaso is not a great defensive player, relying instead on his bat to get him in the lineup. Unfortunately, his bat—swung from the left side—only

---

*In 2012, he was paid the minimum—$492,000. In 2013, he was eligible for arbitration and his salary would nearly quadruple. In December 2015, he signed a two-year, eight-million-dollar contract with the Pittsburgh Pirates. By any reasonable judgment, he is a rich young man. Among major league players, he is a pauper.

seems to work against right-handed pitchers, further lim-
iting his opportunities. But he rakes right-handers and
will undoubtedly stay in the big leagues for a good while,
as long as he can perform passably behind the plate as
well as beside it. If anyone should seek every advantage, it
would be a player like him.

So what does he do in the scout meetings? Not much.
He asks who's been hot and pretty much leaves it at that.

"There's been enough trial and error throughout your
career," he said. "It's like a doctor going into surgery. Is
he going to open up his books and retake the course? Is a
book going to tell him how to open up a heart better than
his experience doing it? That's one of the worst things you
can do on a baseball field, is think. You just have to let it
happen.

"I'm not a believer in watching tape. Not at all. You
can look at some of these guys, say [Jason] Varitek,[9] he
was pretty well known for studying tape. I think it's just
eyewash, personally. A pitcher sees he really cares about
his job. I think that's all it's doing. I don't think it's doing
anything to benefit his game whatsoever. I would say,
maybe, look at some stuff. I would look at stat sheets and
see who's been hot the last five games, who's been hot the
last ten games, and see what they've been doing, if they've
been hitting homers or not. If Prince Fielder[10] is not hot,
I'm not going to go look at tape and see he's been hitting
this pitch out of the park. . . . A-Rod is not catching up
to the fastball. I would just go right at him. You could
get carried away with it. Say he was swinging and missing on curveballs. Say you've got a pitcher in the game,

and curveball is not his best pitch, or it's not even a good pitch. I wouldn't want to do that. I'd want to go with the pitcher's strengths. I'd go to the pitcher's strengths first and work backward from there. You got to see what the pitcher is bringing that day."[11]

That day in the bullpen, warming up before the game, Hernandez looked sharp. Like many pitchers, he was often at his worst early in games, needing an inning or two to catch the game's rhythm. It often didn't seem to matter that much how the bullpen warm-up session went. Some days, great warm-ups were followed by terrible performance. Still, Willis, the pitching coach, nodded his approval as Hernandez threw. "That's some good stuff right there, buddy," he told his pitcher.[12] Hernandez felt it, too.

"As soon as I come out for that game, I know I have something going on, because all of the pitches were working and I could throw any pitch in any count," Hernandez said.[13]

IT SOUNDED LOW

Hernandez has a good time at the ballpark. He came to the big leagues as just a kid, and in many ways has stayed a kid. He looks the part. He's a big guy, but wears even bigger clothes; they look like hand-me-downs he hasn't quite grown into. He jokes with opposing players, especially with fellow Latinos. When pitching against guys he knows, he talks to them from the mound. When he takes the field on game days at home, he skips sideways across the foul line en route, a sort of playful little jig. He's not going to work. He's going out to have some fun.*

It's not likely to be quite so much fun for the opposing hitters. In one recent survey of the best pitchers in baseball—who has the best fastball, best curve, etc.—he was ranked in three different categories. A pitcher can survive in the majors having just one superior pitch; to have three is almost unfair. A broadcaster once asked him what his best pitch was. All five, he said.

It wasn't that way when Hernandez first came up to the big leagues. He arrived with an overpowering fastball, throwing up to 98 mph. He was a straight power pitcher.

Early baseball was a hitter's sport. Hitters could request pitchers to throw the ball in specific locations. Teams routinely scored dozens of runs, sometimes as many as one hundred. Pitchers were placed inside a box about forty feet from the hitters and were required to throw the ball underhanded. They were also supposed to throw the ball as slowly as possible. To ensure the speed limit was adhered to, the pitcher was required to keep his wrist stiff. The rule makers might as well have served the ball to hitters on a platter, which was exactly the point. The rule specified: "The ball must be pitched, not thrown, for the bat."[14] It was more like slow-pitch softball, or coach-pitch Little League, than the game we know today.

---

*It brings to mind the line of Willie Stargell, a slugger for the Pittsburgh Pirates in the 1970s: "The umpire," Stargell liked to say, "yells 'Play ball,' not 'Work ball.'"

It didn't take long—the first year? the first month? who knows, the first game?—before pitchers started bending the rules.

The simplest way to think of the motion of throwing a ball is to see it as a series of levers connected by a series of hinges—the shoulder, the elbow, the wrist, the knuckles of the pitching hand. Given the circumstances required of them—underhanded toss from within a circumscribed area—the most obvious way to subvert the rules was to cheat on the wrist-hinge prohibition. The point was to throw it harder. Who could even tell if the wrist was straight?

So the fastball became baseball's first deliberate pitch—its first pitch, really, and almost certainly its first illegal pitch. As pitchers took more and more liberties with the rules, their disobedience was finally codified in 1885, when overhand, wrist-hinged pitches were finally allowed. This was the most momentous rule change in the game's history, before or since. With it came the modern game. The focus of the entire sport changed to the pitcher-hitter confrontation, and pitchers became huge stars. Instead of setting the table for hitters, they now became fierce and frightening. They didn't merely throw fastballs. Those fastballs took on great metaphorical weight. They threw heat. They threw peas and seeds. They threw cheese—sometimes high cheese, sometimes cheddar. They threw gas, smoke, and hum. They could even throw with mustard or make chin music.

It is often said by baseball fans and practitioners that hitting a baseball is the hardest single task in any sport. Maybe, maybe not. I for one would rather try to hit Aroldis Chapman's 101 mph fastball than have a 330-pound defensive tackle collide with my rib cage at a full sprint. And returning an Andy Roddick 150 mph serve doesn't seem like a simple thing to do, either. But there wouldn't even be a discussion of this without the 1885 rule change.

There has been a long and ferocious debate about the origins of baseball, with the overwhelming consensus that, no, Abner Doubleday, a Union Army officer, did not invent the game in Elihu Phinney's cow pasture in Cooperstown, New York, in 1839. Games had been played with bats and balls before the United States itself was born. These games varied widely over time and terrain. The historian John Thorn for a long while credited the invention to a trio of men who set and codified the rules of the modern game in the middle 1850s.[15] Whoever actually set down the rudiments of the game, it was the change thirty-odd years later allowing pitchers to pitch that set the game on its forward path.

Pitch speed has since been one of baseball's most prized commodities. The reason is straightforward. Although big league hitters have such great hand-eye coordination that they can time almost any pitch if they know it's coming, speed gives an advantage to the pitcher that simply never goes away. It makes everything a hitter has to do harder, because speed steals time from the hitter and time is the hitter's scarcest asset. Even if the hitter expects a fastball and gets one, the harder it is thrown, the less time he has to catch up to it. The faster it is thrown, the quicker it arrives. Guys who throw the hardest have the biggest advantage. The difference in time available to a hitter between a 90 mph fastball and one thrown at 100 mph is approximately forty milliseconds. That doesn't sound like much, but it represents a 10 percent cut in the time allowed to the hitter—time a hitter can't afford to lose. You can see this in the way hitters react to the supreme power pitchers. Mainly, they don't make much contact. Johnny Evers, the great Chicago second baseman of "Tinker to Evers to Chance" fame,* said that the success of hard throwers "proves that the batter does not hit at the ball at all, but swings his bat at a spot where he expects the ball to cross the plate. The success of the fast ball lies in this, and in the fact that it is coming so rapidly the batter has no opportunity to change the direction of his swing before the ball passes."[16]

If you've never been in close proximity to a major league fastball, it can upon first exposure be an unsettling experience. The average, traditional fastball thrown today travels at about 91 to 92 mph. Next time you go to a ball game, go early and stand in the aisle above the bull-pen to watch pitchers warm up. Or listen as they warm up. You can actually hear the ball as it goes by. It hisses like an arrow and hits the catcher's mitt not with a thud but with the sharp crack of a shot from a high-powered sniper rifle.† It's true that the pitch doesn't move much in

---

* For those whose historical recall might have faded, Joe Tinker, Johnny Evers, and Frank Chance were highly regarded infielders with the Chicago Cubs in the early years of the twentieth century. The refrain "Tinker to Evers to Chance" was part of a poem, "Baseball's Sad Lexicon" by Franklin Pierce Adams, first published in 1910, that described the deadly regularity with which the Cubs turned ground balls into double plays.

† If anyone on those Mariner teams of the late eighties could actually have thrown a real fastball, poor Cary would never have napped so well in left field. The racket would have kept everybody awake.

any direction other than forward: most four-seamers are as straight as a Kansas two-lane. Still, standing in the box whether the pitch was straight or not, you could imagine being wounded by it. Or killed.

Walter Johnson, the greatest fastball pitcher of all time, was one of the few successful pitchers in MLB history who threw the fastball and, until late in a long career, almost nothing else. He won 417 games, so it's hard to argue with his approach. Most mortals can't do that.

The story is told[17] that during a late-afternoon game in Washington, D.C.'s old Griffith Stadium, a hitter took a pitch from Johnson for a called strike two. The hitter complained to the umpire:

"That sounded low," he said, then turned and headed for the dugout.*

"That's only two," the umpire called after him. "You've got another strike coming."

The batter, who had had enough of both Johnson and the ump, told him: "Take it yourself," and continued on his way to the dugout.

The same was said of Sandy Koufax, the Dodger ace of the 1960s. Gene Mauch, a longtime major league manager, called Koufax's fastball a radio ball—"a pitch you hear, but you don't see." Richie Ashburn, a Hall of Fame center fielder for the Phillies, said: "Either he throws the fastest ball I've ever seen, or I'm going blind."

Through the course of baseball history, most of the pitching heroes after Johnson were, like him, hard throw-

---

*The noise that Johnson's fastball made was the main reason for his nickname, Big Train, applied to him by the sportswriter Grantland Rice.

ers. There have, of course, been exceptions—the most obvious recent example being Greg Maddux, who won 355 games, mostly for the Atlanta Braves in a two-decade career that ended in 2008. But an overwhelming majority of dominant pitchers—think Bob Feller, Satchel Paige, Lefty Grove, Bob Gibson, Koufax, Nolan Ryan, Roger Clemens, and a host of others[18]—made their careers based on overwhelming fastballs. It is the pitch that all by itself establishes a pitcher as a potential star—a kid with a golden arm. Feller came straight off an Iowa farm* to Major League stardom as a seventeen-year-old and was virtually unhittable.

TOP OF THE FIRST

Speed is, in a sense, stupid. It doesn't have to be anything other than what it is. If you have it, you don't have to have much else. Possessing a great fastball, as Bill James described it, is more a matter of natural talent than practiced skill. Hernandez was born with it. When he was first called up to the Mariners in 2005, he had immediate success as a nineteen-year-old, throwing his fastball in the high 90s. Then throwing his fastball in the high 90s. Then throwing his fastball . . . Well, you get the picture.

Even with his ample inheritance, if that's all you throw,

---

*The myth of the farm boy pitcher is not entirely unfounded. Before Feller, Walter Johnson, Grover Cleveland Alexander, and Cy Young were notable for their rural roots. But baseball had its beginnings as a city game, and professional baseball has always been urban just because getting people to buy tickets means you have to locate teams where there are people.

unless you're Walter Big Train Johnson, you're going to get lit up. Hitters know what they're going to get, and they sit there and wait for it.

Hernandez was fast, but not dumb. He quickly developed more pitches. It seemed he added something new every year. Even as his repertoire grew, however, he stubbornly privileged the weapon that had brought him to the majors—the fastball. Especially early in games, he tended to throw almost nothing but fastballs, presumably because his control of his developing off-speed pitches was insufficient. This tendency reached such a point that David Cameron, a Seattle blogger, wrote an open letter to the Mariners' pitching coach begging him to intervene.[19]

In Hernandez's third season, Cameron had begun charting his pitches. This is a standard practice on major league teams; people have been doing it for decades.[20] It wasn't then so standard for fans to do it, too. Baseball bloggers have done a lot of stuff that no one expected, including some of the most incisive analysis and commentary that exists. In any event, Cameron was appalled to see that Hernandez was throwing upward of 90 percent fastballs in his first inning of work. Hitters were hitting it, too. The first inning was by far the worst in a typical Hernandez start.

The coach showed Cameron's letter to Hernandez, telling him that if a local blogger knew what pitches he was going to throw, surely major league hitters could figure it out, too. That was in 2007. Much has changed since. Hernandez is now routinely described as one of the elite pitchers in baseball and one with phenomenal stuff, "stuff" being a vague concept loosely meaning he throws hard and throws crooked when he needs to, too.

So what happened in the first that August afternoon against the Rays? He threw seven pitches, six of them fastballs. Three up, three down. Who needs deception?

The year before, Hernandez had explained his approach: "I'm a smart pitcher. I'm a hard thrower who knows what he has to do. I know myself and go by my strengths and not by the guys who are hitting. . . . I'm thinking on every pitch that I need to throw—every pitch has to have a purpose—but I don't like to watch any video or look at scouting reports. I know the other guys in the league. I know what they can hit and what they can't. If they can't hit a fastball, I have to throw a fastball. But if he's killing the fastball, can I not throw a fastball? No. It's my best pitch, so I have to throw it."[21]

Hernandez came into the league throwing a traditional four-seam fastball, so called because it's gripped across the seams and spins in such a way that the hitter sees the rotation of all four seams of the ball.* It spins from bottom to top, causing it to rise, compared to a normal trajectory. This is what is meant when players talk about a fastball hopping or rising. It appears to them to be rising because the brain computes a trajectory for the pitch by assuming a normal downward tilt. Every pitch, no matter what type or who throws it, sinks somewhat en route from the pitcher to the hitter. For one thing, pitches are thrown with a raised arm downhill from a small mound and aimed still lower, the top of the strike zone being about

---

*A baseball actually has only one seam, a continuous double stitch that is shaped like a cartoon dog bone—two bulbous ends connected by a narrower middle section.

four feet high. Gravity pulls pitches farther toward earth. The net result is that an average fastball descends about three feet. The slower the pitch, the longer it is in the air, so the more gravity is able to draw it down. No one throws with escape velocity, but a faster pitch, especially one with backspin to combat the gravitational pull, will rise relative to how much the hitter thought it would fall. The best of them rise as much as a foot above the expected trajectory. The four-seamer is almost always the fastest pitch in a pitcher's arsenal.

Sam Fuld was the leadoff hitter for the Tampa Bay Rays. Fuld is a speedy, slight, defensively gifted outfielder who has never been able to win a job as a full-time major league player. He was drafted by the Chicago Cubs out of Stanford, where he actually earned a degree in economics—rare among Division 1 college athletes—and excelled in the Cubs' minor league system, yet could never win a roster spot on the big club. He came to the Rays in a trade in 2011 and has been a backup player for them since.[22] He's a contact hitter without much power. It's this last point that dictates how the Mariners will attack him.

Since he was the first hitter, the bases were empty, obviously. Jaso, the catcher, played with Fuld the previous season, when both were with Tampa. They're good friends, but have almost opposite approaches to the game. Fuld is one of surprisingly few MLB players who have spent much time studying advanced statistics. He actually pays attention to the extensive scouting reports the Rays' staff prepares for each game's pitcher.

"We're given a lot of information and it's up to us what we do with it," he said. "The hitting coach breaks down

what he throws pitch by pitch, what he throws with runners in scoring position, heat maps for locations, handedness breakdown. Most guys kind of keep to the basics. I
look a little deeper," he said.[23]

What he knows foremost from studying the charts
about Hernandez is what Cameron the blogger knew, and
what everybody who doesn't study the charts knows—that
his great fastball is his most hittable pitch. The off-speed
arsenal Hernandez has developed since his first three years
in the league are now his dominant weapons.

Jaso, of course, knows all this, too. But for him, an
awful lot of baseball is purely instinctual. All he needed
to know about his friend Fuld he could gather by looking
at him as he walked up to the plate. Fuld is five feet nine
inches tall and weighs maybe 170 pounds. By 2012, he
had four career home runs.

"Obviously, we go right after him," Jaso said.

Hernandez threw a 92 mph fastball at the top of the
strike zone and got a generous strike call from the home
plate umpire, Rob Drake.* He then threw the same pitch
and missed, followed that with a lazy curve that he was
lucky also missed, up and away. Neither the pitcher nor
the catcher had any fear of Fuld whatsoever, although he
had gone 2-for-4 against Hernandez earlier in the year.

"That's the way pitchers pitch to little guys," Fuld said.
"That's generally my strategy, especially with him—look
for a fastball I don't like to swing at first pitch of the game,

---

* Umpires are scrutinized as much as players. They, too, have their tendencies
and peculiar notions of what is a strike and what is a ball. Drake is in the
middle of the pack, not regarded as a pitcher's or a hitter's ump.

so I took it. When I get to 0-1, now you have to be more aware of the off-speed stuff."[24]

When the count got to 2-1, Fuld was sitting on Hernandez's fastball, and that's what he got. He drove the ball hard into the right-center-field gap. The Mariner right fielder Eric Thames, a fading prospect whose search for a big league career eventually carried him to Korea, took a shaky route to the ball but outran it and made the catch on the dead run with his back to home.[25]

It's worth noting here that Safeco is a miserable park to hit in. For much of the year, the air is heavy and damp and the temperature is a consistent ten degrees cooler than elsewhere in the baseball-playing world. Robert Adair, a physicist with an interest in baseball, has found that a ten-degree increase in air temperature means four extra feet of batted ball distance.[26] The greater the temperature spread, the more depressing the effect is. Seattle is a good place to be a pitcher.

"I hit that ball about as well as I can hit a ball," Fuld said. "In a lot of ballparks it's off the wall or even a home run. I crushed that ball. I was really surprised, given the setting, that it was still caught. I was like, 'Okay.' You're never happy when you get out, but I put a good swing on it."[27]

B. J. Upton, the Rays' center fielder, hit next. Upton is one of the most gifted athletes in the major leagues—fast, lithe, strong. He has been expected to become a star since he came into the league, but has remained inconsistent, a good enough hitter but nowhere near one of the best. Jaso regards him as someone to be wary of—"a guy who

can hurt you with one swing of the bat"—but a hitter you can attack.[28]

No hitter really likes to face a pitcher like Hernandez, somebody who can make you look silly. "Going to be a tough four ABs today," Upton told Jaso as he settled into the box. Thinking about the remark later, Jaso was amused, saying, "He only got three."

Upton was looking first-pitch fastball and swung at one outside and high. Unluckily for him, he made contact, sending a slow hopper up the middle, where the shortstop, Brendan Ryan, as good a defender as there was in baseball, scooped it up and threw easily to first to get Upton.

Up third was Matt Joyce, a left-handed hitter with some power. Like Upton, he's a promising young player who has yet to deliver on the promise. Hernandez, almost disdainful, threw him two fastballs, the first up and away, the second up. Joyce swung at the second and hit an easy roller to the second baseman, Dustin Ackley, for the third out.

Hernandez threw seven pitches, six of them identical four-seamers, up, in, or out of the strike zone. They ranged in speed from 92 to 94 mph and had average to below-average movement. But the Rays, knowing that Hernandez had been on a terrific run all summer, were eager—too eager—to avoid getting behind on Hernandez, and swung at pitches early in the count.

It was just the first inning, and already Hernandez was in their heads.

THE CURVEBALL

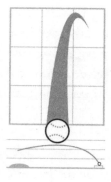

SWEET AS CANDY

Pitchers, being more or less human,* are greedy. As soon as they were allowed—with a wink and a smile—to throw the ball hard, they began to experiment with ways to throw it not just hard but crooked, too.

---

*Human, but not regarded by their teammates as members of quite the same species. In conversation, nonpitchers regularly divide their teams between players and pitchers, the pitchers apparently not being qualified as players. The odd part of this is that pitchers are often among the best athletes on a team. It's the hitters who have the far more idiosyncratic skill. There are dozens of major league pitchers who began their careers as hitters. The number who traveled in the opposite direction—from pitcher to hitter—is vanishingly small. The very large exception, of course, is the greatest hitter in the history of the sport—Babe Ruth.

The game then was played in a style nothing like its profligate contemporary descendant. For one important difference, there was the ball itself. Then a whole game might be played with a half-dozen balls.* Balls would quickly become dirty, scuffed, out of round.

Contemporary major league balls are made according to strict specifications in a single factory in Turrialba, a small town in the Costa Rican interior. It is a very complicated little product. The ball weighs about five ounces and is approximately nine inches around, more or less the size of your fist. It has a cork center, wrapped in two thin layers of rubber, then wound tightly with wool yarn. To be precise, it is wound with 121 yards of blue-gray wool yarn, 45 yards of white yarn, 53 more yards of blue-gray yarn, and 150 yards of a fine white poly-wool blend. Only then is it finally covered in two pieces of figure-eight-shaped white cowhide leather,† which has been tanned in Tennessee and shipped to the Costa Rican factory. Once the winding is

---

*When I was young, my semipro town team would buy a dozen dozen balls in the spring and expect not to have exhausted the supply by fall. This meant, of course, that foul balls were retrieved from fans, often at some risk to the retriever. One of my first jobs was as ball chaser. Today, with balls being dismissed from play every time they touch dirt, and with fielders tossing them willy-nilly into the stands as souvenirs, a typical major league game can consume that dozen dozen in a single evening. The average is about 120 balls per game.

† Horsehide, the original cover and the source of infield chatter to throw the old horsehide, hasn't been used since 1974, when the switch—because of chronic shortages of horsehide—was made; horsehide disappeared, gone the way of the chatter. For all the noise in contemporary ballparks, almost none of it comes from the players, who go about their business in stoic silence. It's strange, in part because ballplayers are generally a talkative bunch. They have a lot of downtime in the clubhouse, on the field before games, in buses and planes, and they fill a lot of it by talking relentlessly at and with one another. Maybe, by the time the game starts, they're tired of talking.

complete, the ball is wrapped in the shiny white leather and held together by 108 hand-sewed double stitches, consuming 88 inches of thick red cotton thread.

The balls are rolled between steel platens to flatten but not wholly eliminate the red seams, leaving the seams raised about .03 inch. The balls leave the factory as perfect and shiny as fresh-cut diamonds. The shine, a product of the tanning process the cowhide has undergone, is removed at each major league park, where, before games, the balls are rubbed with mud dredged from the bottom of the Delaware River.* Removing the shine has little effect on the ball beyond allowing the pitcher to get a more consistent grip on it.

The general result of the manufacturing process is an object much more uniform in dimension and predictable in trajectory than anything earlier generations had used.

Considering the physical nature of baseballs in the formative years of the game, it came as no surprise to anyone that a ball could be made to go in something other than a straight line. Any kid who's ever skipped a rock across a pond knows how much easier it is to curve a lopsided rock than one perfectly formed. It's a wonder anyone could ever throw those old balls straight. They were irregular at best, even when new.

The claims as to who threw the ball crookedest soonest

---

*Exactly where on the Delaware River in New Jersey remains a closely held secret for reasons too mysterious to fathom. Do they think somebody will steal all the mud? The mud has a name, perhaps the only mud in the world with one: Lena Blackburne Baseball Rubbing Mud. Blackburne discovered the mud near his New Jersey home when he was a third-base coach for the Philadelphia Athletics, then marketed it to the American League.

are many and conflicting, but there is little doubt that, even before it was legal to fool hitters, plenty of pitchers were trying to do exactly that. The most consistent claims for the first pitcher to perfect a deliberately curved pitch have been made by, and on behalf of, a little guy named Arthur "Candy" Cummings, the nickname bestowed by an admiring manager who pronounced his stuff sweet.

Cummings promoted himself as the inventor of the breaking ball, saying he'd been inspired by throwing clam-shells along the Massachusetts shore as a boy and dreamed of throwing a baseball with the same outrageous curva-ture.[1] He gripped the ball tightly at the end of his fingers and, illegally, snapped his wrist as he released the pitch. Pitching in amateur leagues in the 1860s, the five-foot-six, 120-pound pitcher worked to gain consistent con-trol of the curveball. Some days he had it, others not. He began to wear a glove on his pitching hand to ward off the blisters he got from what he referred to as the death grip needed to throw his curve. It's not entirely clear what advantage could be gained from such a tight hold on the ball; contemporary pitching instructors would argue that a tighter grip reduces rather than encourages spin on a thrown ball.

Nobody knows exactly what magic Cummings con-jured to make his ball curve. He threw lopsided balls underhanded, so whatever he did surely differed from the modern game. He was secretive about developing the pitch, thinking—rightly—that it would give him a com-petitive advantage. At his diminutive size, he figured, he needed every advantage he could find. He claimed that he had his first real success when he discovered gripping

the ball with only the ends of his fingers, then snapping his wrist just as he released the ball. Cummings was not a complete outlier. Pitchers of the era routinely broke rules in an attempt to get something closer to equal standing with hitters, who were allowed to request where in the hitting zone they would like a pitch to be delivered.[2]

Cummings bounced around the semipro and amateur ranks, as was common in those early years, taking whatever offer was most advantageous. Eventually, he was signed by the big league New York Mutuals of the National Association in 1872 and racked up thirty-three wins against twenty losses in what for the era was a not unusual fifty-five games pitched.* He continued to change teams almost annually, and provided sterling results. His career earned run average was 2.42, excellent in any era.

Cummings's monopoly on the curveball, if it ever existed, was short-lived. He had learned to manipulate the early rules outlawing almost everything a pitcher might do to gain advantage, but by 1877—his last year as an elite player—many of the restrictions were removed, and bigger, stronger pitchers took the mound. Cummings was out of the big leagues by the end of 1877. The art of deception that he helped initiate had just begun.

---

*A contemporary starting pitcher will appear in about thirty-four games. Cummings's total was not at all unusual for the era. Before 1900, it wasn't unheard of for a pitcher to throw in almost all of his team's games, more than seventy games in a season. These were not normally brief appearances, either. In those years, pitchers were expected to complete what they started—relief pitchers hadn't really been invented yet. In the nineteenth century, at least six pitchers threw at least seventy complete games in single seasons. Dozens threw more than fifty complete games. Pitchers routinely threw five or six hundred innings, double or triple what contemporary pitchers achieve. Today five or six complete games will lead the league most years.

The move to overhand throwing was but the first major change in major league pitching. It advantaged pitchers to an almost unconscionable degree. Allowing pitchers to throw overhand, and hard, from a box fifty feet from the plate must have felt unfair, mainly because it was. It is an unreasonably difficult task to hit a major league fastball thrown from the contemporary distance—sixty feet six inches.[3] From fifty feet on the run it was nearly impossible.

The second great change occurred to address the inequity the first rule change had created. Pitchers had gone from being mere servants to the batters to their overwhelming masters. The pitching distance was moved back five feet at a time until 1893, when the current distance was established. As important as the increased distance was the elimination of the pitcher's box, which was replaced by a small slab, what we know today as the pitching rubber. Instead of being allowed to run at the hitter before throwing the pitch—similar to what occurs in cricket—the pitcher was in a fixed location. The distance of the rubber from home plate—sixty feet six inches—had no special significance; it was just where the mound ended up after a series of moves. By chance, it had landed at what now seems the best distance, the only imaginable distance, it so happens, from which pitchers can manipulate the path of the ball as they do. Think about it. Most breaking balls break appreciably more when they lose speed. They lose speed as they advance toward the plate. From fifty feet, a knuckleball wouldn't knuckle, a curveball might curve but not much, a sinker wouldn't sink. From sixty feet six inches, it can be made to do all of those things and more.

If the mound were any other distance from the plate,

the basic dynamic of the pitcher-hitter confrontation would be utterly different; it might even disappear. The decision to set this distance was almost providential, a good break for the future of baseball.

Once the distance was set and the pitching rubber established,* pitchers, often without really knowing how or why the ball would move, embarked on a prolonged investigation of how to manipulate pitches. It became a subject of some fascination among the public. A Pennsylvania newspaper, the *Reading Eagle,* in 1891 published a column on its front page quoting John Clarkson of the Boston Beaneaters on how to throw a curveball: "He wants to fool the other fellows when they come to the bat. He cannot be blamed for that. . . . Let the young aspirant grasp the ball firmly in his hand. Giving the pressure with his forefinger and middle finger. The other two fingers should be drawn in towards the palm. Next let him snap the ball out of one side of the hand, and the next one out of the other."

One of the great early practitioners of the curveball was Mordecai "Three Finger" Brown, so called because as an Indiana farm boy he had lost a finger and a half to a feed chopper. The resulting disfigured but still-capable pitching hand enabled him—almost unbidden—to impart incredible spin to the ball. His overhand curve—called

---

*The contemporary pitching rubber is six inches deep and twenty-four inches wide. It is set slightly to the rear of center of the mound, which is no higher than ten inches tall. A pitcher's foot is supposed to stay in contact with the rubber until he releases the ball. This is honored more in theory than in practice. Some pitchers habitually lose contact with the rubber while pushing forward in their pitching motion.

a drop or a hook—made him one of the most dominant pitchers of the era. Brown pitched mainly for the Chicago Cubs in the first two decades of the twentieth century. He was frequently matched against the seemingly invincible Christy Mathewson, and was the best big-game pitcher of his time. Ty Cobb, the greatest hitter of baseball's early era, called Brown's curve the "most devastating" pitch he had to face. Brown became sufficiently renowned that he was commissioned to write a series of newspaper articles—"How to Pitch a Curve"—that was repackaged into a book.

The curveball quickly became a standard part of the pitching repertoire, the first in what would become an armory of off-speed weapons pitchers could deploy.

Candy Cummings's curveball, because he was a right-hander throwing more or less sidearm, almost certainly broke dramatically right-to-left, but probably didn't move much vertically. This type of curve, often called a round-house curve, can have tremendous movement from side to side. It starts off seemingly aimed behind the back of a right-handed hitter, then curves all the way across the batter's box and finishes on the outside part of the plate. Twenty years later, in the days of Mordecai Brown, this side-to-side movement gave way to pitches that dropped dramatically down. This is the curve in its most devastating form. Thrown almost directly overhand, and falling sharply as much as a foot pretty much straight down as it reaches home plate, it is virtually unhittable. In general, pitches that break vertically are more consistently difficult to hit than pitches that break horizontally. The reason is straightforward. A ball that moves side to side remains largely on the same plane throughout its flight, similar to the movement of a bat through the strike zone. There is almost no room for error for a hitter on pitches breaking vertically. Willie Stargell famously said that facing Sandy Koufax's overhand curve was like trying to drink coffee with a fork.

Brown was the early master of the straight overhand pitch. In later eras, the pitch acquired different names— the yakker, the yellow hammer, the deuce, the hook, Uncle Charlie, Lord Charles, and, most recently, Public Enemy Number One. The latter term was applied by Vin Scully, the legendary Los Angeles Dodger play-by-play man, to describe the current Dodger southpaw Clayton Kershaw's curve. The nickname "deuce" comes from the typical signal a catcher uses to ask the pitcher to throw a curve. The catcher signals the pitch he would like the pitcher to throw (sometimes relaying the manager's decision) by waggling fingers between his thighs while in a catcher's customary crouch. For decades, it has been common for catchers to signal for a fastball by waggling one finger, and two fingers for a curve—hence the deuce. From there, signals get more complicated: many catcher-pitcher combinations vary in how they call for other pitches.

"The hook" is self-explanatory. "Lord Charles" was the name given in the 1980s to young Dwight Gooden's curveball when he first came to the majors. Teammates thought his curve was so superior to others that the more common nickname then in use—Uncle Charlie—was insufficiently plebeian. I've no idea where "Uncle Charlie" came from, but it's been in use for seventy years. "Yakker" and "yellow hammer" have both been said to derive from the flight of a particular woodpecker.*

Bob Feller, Herb Score, Camilo Pascual, Barry Zito, Kerry Wood, Sal Maglie, Orel Hershiser, and Sandy Koufax were great curveball pitchers. Among contemporary pitchers, Kershaw, Jon Lester, Adam Wainwright, Zack Greinke, Justin Verlander, Aaron Sele, Roy Oswalt, and Chris Carpenter have had great overhand curves, but it is an increasingly rare pitch.

Bert Blyleven, who became an elite pitcher with the Minnesota Twins in the 1970s, has at various times been identified as the best curveballer ever. He was perplexed at his own success. "You can teach anyone to throw it," he said. "I don't know what made mine better other than the proper mechanics. The key is to get your fingers above the ball."[4]

As good as Blyleven was, Koufax was in a class apart. Mickey Mantle, after striking out on a Koufax curve in the 1963 World Series, complained afterward: "How in the fuck are you supposed to hit that shit?"[5] The answer, Mick, is: You're not.

Koufax might or might not have had the best curve of all time, but there is little debate that he had the best combination of fastball-curveball. He could have won with the fastball alone. Looking back at that 1963 series, in which Koufax was dominant, the Yankees' catcher, Yogi Berra,

---

*I have my doubts. I think baseball players, fans, and writers have a lot of time on their hands. It seems plausible that for "yakker" the most likely and pleasing explanation is that a great curve makes batters talk to themselves, which is better perhaps than its alternative—that being silence and forlorn despair.

took note of Koufax's regular season won-loss record of 25-5: "I can understand how he won 25. How the hell did he lose five?" The Dodgers' shortstop, Maury Wills, explained: "He didn't. We lost them for him."[6]

The overhand curve is thrown less these days, in large part because it's hard to get umpires to call it a strike. A good overhand curve breaks from a batter's waist to his knees or below as it crosses the plate. It often ends up in the dirt before a catcher can glove it. Umps look silly calling strikes on balls in the dirt, and umps don't like to look silly. David Wells pitched for nine teams over twenty-one years, ending in 2007, mainly because he could get called strikes on his overhand curve.[7]

LOW AND AWAY

I saw my first breaking ball in a barnyard. It came from my cousin Kenny, and in the dusty twilight I was helpless. When the ball came, it was aimed directly at my head. Or so it seemed. My knees quivered and buckled, the way they do when your body disobeys your brain. I fell back out of the batter's box, then stood helplessly as the ball sliced past, nicking the outside corner of the plate—a plank end, actually—and plunked into the backstop, an empty feed sack hanging in the doorway of the hog barn. I blamed the twilight, but I almost certainly would have been helpless at noon. Boy, was I a terrible hitter.

Kenny, the silent type, smiled his slim gunslinger smile, so slight you wondered what it was he knew that you didn't. That never changed in him. He hid things, ambitions, abilities. I wished Howie, out at shortstop, had the same restraint. He did not. Kenny was a secret; Howie was a hustler. He hid nothing. When I swung and missed, he would shout with glee: "C'mon, Monica, hit the ball."

Monica—yes, that Monica!—lived not far up the road; she and her twin, Veronica, were the only girls my age Howie knew, so he thought teasing me about them was a good way to get me. He was right. My sunburned face would glow still brighter in the gloaming, and I'd fire the ball back to Kenny and dig in again.

The barnyard tilted uphill away from the pigpen and home plate. So Kenny pitched from the equivalent of a mound, downhill. Howie made me mad, and I'd squeeze the bat handle and imagine hitting the ball out past the windmill in center, all the way out to where Blackie, the three-legged dog, lounged against the fence. His work for the day, bringing the cows in for milking morning and night, was done. He lounged in left center. He was not much worried I would disturb him.

I didn't. My hitting days, such as they were, were years away. Then I was a slight, nearly emaciated town kid sent to the farm for the summer with little chance of hitting anything other than a horsefly. In the hours after the wheat, the hay, or the corn harvest of that particular day had been done, the long fade of the sun from the high summer sky gave us our only off hours, and baseball filled a lot of it. I had little choice in the matter. My father, a strict man, had ordered that I love baseball. Except for the odd occasions—say, the time we shot out the living room window from inside the house with a BB gun*—we were generally obedient children, and we obeyed. So we played baseball and were happy for the command to do so.

My town was in eastern Iowa, hundreds of miles in any direction from major league teams. The White Sox and Cubs were nearest, and each had its local fans. My father rooted for the Yankees. In basketball, he rooted for the Boston Celtics, and in football the Green Bay Packers. I sense a pattern here. This was the 1960s. He had an eye for quality, or a weakness for winning, perhaps both. Whatever the cause, these were our ordained family teams.

In an early rebellion, I broke from the Packers, choosing instead the Chicago Bears of Rick Casares and Willie Galimore. It's not as if I was objecting to my father's frontrunning. The Bears won the NFL title in 1963, my first year as a declared fan. I stuck with the Yankees through their long decline in the late sixties but lost touch with the team when I joined the Air Force and was stationed in Vietnam for a year. I drifted away from baseball entirely, and from almost everything else in the mainstream of American life over the next few years. Still, I took my glove with me wherever I moved, including that sojourn in Saigon. I played fast-pitch softball there for the first time, and also for the first time learned to dive for cover when the Vietnamese Army guards in the towers along the outfield fence decided it was time to play Yankee Go Home and would swing their machine guns toward the

---

*The responsibility for this misdeed is still being argued. It's true it was my gun and at some point I had my finger on the trigger, but let's just say there was an attempt at intervention that did not go as planned. If I'd been under my own care, I'm certain the trigger would never have been pulled.

field—rather than away, at the bad guys beyond the Tan Son Nhut perimeter.

The success of the great, late 1970s Bronx Zoo Yankee teams of Thurman Munson, Reggie Jackson, Graig Nettles, and Ron Guidry caused a resurgence for me as a fan, but eventually the owner George Steinbrenner's overbearing personality and inability to stay out of his wonderful team's way wore on me. In the early 1980s, I Martin Luthered George, nailing my complaints about his regime to the op-ed page of an Oregon newspaper. Not that George or anyone else took notice.*

I was living in Portland, Oregon, in those years and sometimes watched games in a Yankee tavern on Southeast Belmont that featured behind the bar a portrait of Munson chasing a foul pop. It was not well rendered. Poor Thurman seemed lost in a cloud that for some reason was green. So was I—lost, that is—although my cloud might have been a different color. I was completely stuck in a life that I realized I had been trying to run from ever since I fled Cascade. When I was a kid, Mac's preferred name for me—when he wasn't accidentally calling me Happy, the dog's name—was Dark Cloud. It was, as usual for his knife work, spot-on. I had been stuck inside some sort of darkness since I could remember. Baseball seemed so much a part of that dark past that I couldn't imagine it

---

*I sense a pattern here: me taking a principled stand that no one notices and nonetheless diving into the deep end of whatever dispute I was then engaged in. There was always something, let me tell you. More than once, the deep end was absent water, and after a while even I learned that ramming your head into the concrete bottom of the pool was not a sustainable practice. Took a while, though.

in my future. The game was old and quaint and rural. I was new and modern and almost certainly about to conquer the known world. (See the footnote to the preceding paragraph about the author's tendency to believe stupid things.) What possible use could baseball be to me?

My interest in the game was revived by, of all things, fantasy baseball. I joined an early fantasy league in Eugene, Oregon, in 1984, and through that stumbled onto Bill James, who then was already years into perhaps the strangest publishing career in American history. Beginning in 1977, James had been self-publishing annual *Baseball Abstracts* that explored the basis of a radical rethinking of baseball analysis. By the time I fell upon him, the *Abstracts* had been transformed into a mainstream enterprise with a big New York publisher and lots of critical acclaim. I didn't care about any of that. I just wanted to win my fantasy league and thought James's analysis was a shortcut to doing my own homework and building my franchise.

Which, of course, it was. The M & M Boys, the team I shared with a friend, Mark Matassa, were unaccountably successful, given our own primitive understanding of how to project what players might be successful in any given year. We had James and we had fantastic luck. Julio Franco, Juan Samuel, and Jesse Barfield blossomed into stars under our tutelage. Well, of course not. But that's how fantasy owners come to think of these things. One of the pursuit's charms and one of its faults.*

---

*These original fantasy leagues have about the same relationship to the contemporary FanDuel and DraftKings gambling enterprises as baseball in Cascade has to the contemporary MLB. That is, they seem to have come from a long time ago and very far away.

In the course of things, I became addicted to fantasy leagues—who has tried it and not?—but I also fell in love with James as a writer, as a skeptic, as an outsider, as a very strange and insightful devotee of a very strange game. James's quirky and unrelenting insights into something I had thought of as static and old inspired an inquiry into the depths of the game I hadn't known existed. It was like a bored and incurious student encountering a great teacher and suddenly discovering that history was a living organism begging to be decoded. I had often joked that baseball was the favored sport of intellectuals because it was so slow even they could understand it. This was meant as a critique but was now transformed into admiration. Baseball rewards attention. It also rewards inattention. It can be enjoyed at whatever level of focus you want to give it. It's like Mac taking me to that cafeteria in downtown Chicago and telling me I could have whatever I wanted. Baseball is a feast laid on a great banquet table. You can have as much or as little as you want. Just stay away from the chicken.

In my case, baseball was graciously slow enough to let me catch up to it after giving it a decade's head start. I had moved to Seattle by 1985, the first place I ever lived that had its own big league team. I started going to games, more as a novelty than out of any passion. I had grown up listening to baseball on the radio, and started to listen again now that I was within range of a major league signal.

I first realized I was falling for the Mariners sometime in the late summer of that year. It was at night—these things always happen at night, don't they? I was alone in a Volkswagen Jetta in the upland desert of eastern Washington, blasting north out of Wapato on U.S. 97, one of the great intermountain highways in the United States. The moon was strobe-light bright, the August air as quiet and still as a penitent.

My first experiences of major league baseball were all on the radio at a time when, as the novelist Mark Harris put it, life itself was slow motion. Before incessant musical recordings began being played in most big league parks, the noise you would hear coming out of the radio during a game (after, of course, the announcers) was the background sounds of the game—vendors chirping out their sales pitches and the communal hum of the crowd. When you hear this on the radio from a thousand miles away, it can come across as some grand Buddhist chant—a prolonged "ommmm." Even though I had lost my nearly religious belief in the game itself, that sound was tucked so deep inside me that, wherever I was, I never quit listening to baseball on the radio. It's like hearing the murmuring of a Latin Mass—however little engagement I had with my Catholic childhood, the ritual chants and the muted call and response still echo inside my head.

I didn't even realize I was missing anything until that night on 97. It was late. The Mariners were losing, and it suddenly occurred to me I didn't care about the game's outcome. I wasn't listening to the game. I was being transported by the hum of the crowd, and, layered over it, I was listening to Dave Niehaus, the Mariner play-by-play guy. Man, what a voice. It insinuated itself into your thoughts even when you didn't know you were listening. The high desert of a moonlit summer night is an enchanting place. When the road was clear and empty, I would turn off my lights and disappear into the darkness of the Horse Heaven Hills.

"The right-hander sets, checks the runners," Niehaus said. "He delivers the 1-2 pitch. Breaking ball." Then came the word that both broke and captured my heart: "Loooooooooowwwwwwwwwww."

That ball-two call stretched out through the Yakima Valley to the Cascades, impossibly deep and long and rich. It soothed. It hurt. It had in it the ache of cattle braying on the plains. It had the idle joy of Niehaus's southern Indiana youth. Harry Caray coming in from St. Louis on KMOX. Watermelon cooling in a No. 10 washtub. Mama's got the sun tea ready. Fireflies flashing. Run to get a Mason jar and jab holes in the lid with an ice pick and welcome those flies to their new home.

Niehaus lived inside a magical world largely of his own creation. He clearly loved baseball, but in many ways it just happened to be what he was given to talk about, that night's stage upon which he could perform. Fans could sense it. They sent him homemade pies and asparagus and Walla Walla onions. Only in Seattle would asparagus be regarded as a great gift. There were also jams and jellies. Boxes of them. Crates of them.

Like all great artists, Niehaus gave the impression that he was artless, that you could do what he does. You could not. Okey-dokey, he'd say, starting the third. That's a can of corn, he'd say, ending the fourth.

Niehaus smoked and drank, probably too much of both. In spring training in Arizona, he presided over a raucous monthlong party at Scottsdale's Pink Pony restaurant. Anybody could join the table. Anybody could stay if they could tell a story. Niehaus loved stories. On the air, you could hear the smoke in his voice—especially in the early innings, as he warmed up. By late night, the bits of gravel in his delivery wore away. He was at his best then, when a tight game found its rhythm and he could fold himself into it. He never tried to overtake the game, but catch it and rolled along inside it. He would lead you conspiratorially, as if offering a hand to guide you through the dark, quietly, murmuring soft and sensuously, carrying you through inconsequential at bats, innings, games, and seasons. Then, all of a sudden, he'd erupt: "My oh my," he'd shout as a ball arced toward the depths. "That will fly away." On the rare occasions when the Mariners hit a grand slam home run, he could barely stay seated as he shouted: "Get out the rye bread and mustard, Grandma, it is grand salami time!"

Being a fan of a bad team is not, contrary to popular opinion circulated mainly by Chicago Cub fans—and what do they know, really?—ennobling. It's far closer to the opposite—abasing. To have a guide as joyful and sublime as Niehaus obscured all that. I crept back into the game. With Niehaus and James, how could I not?

So, by the late 1980s, I was again a full-fledged fan. Niehaus and a new team not tainted by my own past pulled me back in. Unfortunately, my team sucked. Really sucked. Which, of course, they have continued to do now for most of the next three decades.*

---

*We have become so accustomed to losing we can scarcely believe any other outcome is possible. Early last season, 2016, the team, once again under new management, put together an impressive winning string, and a month into

TOP OF THE SECOND

Going against lanky Tampa right-hander Jeremy Hellickson, the Mariners had managed a leadoff single by second baseman Dustin Ackley. Hope was extinguished quickly: he was doubled off, and they got nothing else in their half of the first inning.

Hellickson is in many respects Hernandez's opposite. He came into the league identified as a type often referred to, derisively, as a finesse pitcher. Finesse guys as a rule don't throw very hard, at least not by major league standards; this doesn't mean you would want to face them.

For reasons that remain mysterious, the highest acclaim a pitcher can receive is that he has great "stuff." No one ever says a soft tossing lefty like Jamie Moyer has great stuff,*

---

the season found itself in first place. Cause for celebration, right? Well, of a sort. Here's what one local fan wrote: "For a long time, longer than all of us probably care to remember, the Seattle Mariners have been masters of losing. They have baptized fans in the waters of the River Wallowing, made us drink from the cup of longing and misery, and every time we thought we'd learned our final lesson, they'd found another to teach. The records kept of defeats stretch infinitely back in our minds past the point of actual time. The timelessness we've felt has simply been that Mariners Baseball meant failure and an endless one." We are, as you can see, a group given to darkness. (http://www.lookoutlanding.com/2016/5/10/11647868/felix-sets-mariner-all-time-wins-record-by-winning.)

*Moyer was my favorite Mariner pitcher of all time. He came to the team in 1996, when he was thirty-three, in his tenth big league season, and, incredibly, pitched another fifteen years. He had been advised to retire and become a coach before he ever got to the Mariners, but he won twenty games for the first time when he was thirty-eight and for the second time when he was forty. Felix passed Moyer as the winningest Mariner pitcher of all time in 2016.

although he somehow managed to win 269 games while throwing the ball about as hard as your Aunt Bessie. Why that doesn't count as stuff, I don't know.

In any event, Hellickson's fastball is in the low-90s mph range. Good enough, and faster than most finesse pitchers, but his true weapon is an overhand changeup that completely befuddles hitters. It's one of the best pitches in the league, and the Mariners have had almost no success against it or him. Which might or might not be significant, given that as long as Hellickson has been in the league—since late 2010—the Mariners have been god-awful offensively against everybody.

Being the best pitcher on the worst-hitting team in modern major league history has cost Hernandez countless wins, but he has grown used to this friendly ineptitude by now and almost never complains about it. He is unusual in that he has always mixed freely with the position players. Unusually, Hernandez's best friends on the team have almost always been position players, and he has emerged as a leader of the entire team.

He took the mound to face the middle of the Rays' order, starting with Evan Longoria, the slugging third baseman who was the designated hitter for the Rays that day. Longoria was one of the best players in baseball and the heart of the Rays' offense. He's a big, tough right-handed hitter. Hernandez has owned him, striking Longoria out four out of every ten at bats against him. He's done it mainly by staying away from his fastball. Instead, he throws Longoria a ton of sliders; every third pitch he's thrown to him, in fact, has been a slider.

Tampa hitters, in their pre-game scout meetings, had

been told to be aggressive early in their at bats, to look for Hernandez's fastball and jump on it. This was opposite their normal approach. They were known as a team that took a lot of pitches, running up pitch counts on opposing pitchers. This was a more optimistic way of saying, "Don't let Felix get ahead in the count. He'll kill you." This isn't folk wisdom. In the season 2012 to date, if Hernandez got ahead in the count with his first pitch, opposing batters hit .185 against him. If he got to two strikes, they hit for a .111 average, less than half the overall average (for the season, the league average batting average was .255). By a measurement more favored among contemporary statisticians, OPS (on-base percentage plus slugging percentage), the league was hitting .486 against Hernandez.[8] An individual hitter with those results would not last a week in the big leagues. League average against all pitchers varies year to year, but is usually between .700 and .750. In other words, when facing Hernandez after a first-pitch strike, the best hitters in baseball hit like they don't even belong in the league. No wonder they go to the plate hunting first-pitch fastballs.

So, of course, Hernandez and Jaso started Longoria off with another fastball, above the zone for a ball. If you know, as Hernandez surely does, that everybody coming to the plate is praying you throw him fastballs, why on earth would you do exactly that?

The two cardinal rules of pitching are:

1. Strike one is the most important pitch you can throw; throw strikes.
2. Establish the fastball.

As to the validity of the first rule, there is little doubt. The data declare in the most definitive way possible that pitching ahead in the count—controlling the count, as it's termed today—confers huge advantages to the pitcher. Hitters with an 0-1 count typically perform half as well in that at bat as hitters who take the first pitch for a ball. Hitters who begin an at bat 0-1 hit like pitchers—that is, terribly. It varies year to year, but composite batting average for all hitters in all games when they start out an at bat with a first-pitch strike is about .230. An individual who hits .230 generally has a very short career. Hitters who get ahead in the count 1-0 hit forty points higher, around .275. If you're a pitcher, the message is obvious—throw first-pitch strikes.[9]

As to the validity of the second rule, well, let's just say it's widely but not universally believed.

"If you never throw a fastball, then you're never really changing speeds," said the Mariner pitching coach, Carl Willis. "Everything's soft? Then everything is soft. There has to be a certain number of fastballs in there to keep that balance. I think it's the case. I think that's why you see in so many of his games—and it's not just him [Hernandez], it's whenever any club faces an elite pitcher—you see an awful lot of early swings, because guys want to hit the fastball. They don't want to get into those counts where they're unsure what is coming. Then it becomes a little bit of a guessing game, or hitting that nasty changeup or slider. Whatever the case may be, I do think you still do establish that fastball, and as the game progresses you start to change your sequences."

Here's James Shields, a Tampa Bay righty known not for his fastball but for his great off-speed stuff:

"Fastball command is everything to a pitcher, even if you have a pet pitch like the changeup. . . . I've gotten to the point where I like hitters to be looking for my changeup. In fact, I love it when a guy is up at the plate sitting on my change, because I know that somewhere in the back of his mind, the fact that he's sitting on a changeup makes him uneasy. He knows that waiting for the change will let me easily beat him with my fastball. If a hitter's looking for a pitch that's going to come in around 81 or 82 mph, you can throw him a fastball and it's going to make you look like the second coming of Nolan Ryan. The hitter just doesn't have time to catch up to the pitch."[10]

The fastball-first approach is so ingrained in the major leagues that pitchers who attempt to throw their off-speed pitches early in counts are said to be pitching backward. Major League Baseball is nothing if not normative. Saying someone is pitching backward is not intended as a compliment. As we saw with Hernandez early in his career, there is a limit to how useful it is to start a game throwing all fastballs all the time. Here's the predicament the strategy entangles Hernandez in: to get to his really dynamite off-speed stuff, he has to throw his most hittable pitches exactly when hitters most expect them.

Hernandez has an excellent overhand curveball. The average MLB curveball breaks toward the pitcher's glove side six inches and drops—holding constant for gravity's effect—six inches. Felix is a little better than that, but not hugely. What makes the curve an effective pitch for him is that it is by far his slowest pitch, at 83 mph, providing a genuine velocity difference from his fastball. He uses it almost as a changeup.

He has another, mediocre version of the curveball, of a type that is often called, derisively, a "get me over" curve, a pitch not thrown with any intent other than to surprise a hitter enough in what is ordinarily a fastball count to get a called strike. Hernandez's "get me over" is lazier than his true curve, with a softer, more horizontal break. Jaso describes it as "slurvy," not as fast as a conventional slider and not as much break as a conventional curve. It's not really a weapon, but a plea for restraint: Don't hit me and I won't embarrass you.

This would ordinarily have been the spot for the lesser, "get me over" slurve. Instead, Hernandez snapped off a sharp, 82 mph curve over the outside corner. Longoria took it for a strike.

"He didn't swing at that first fastball or anything, he just tracked it all the way in," Jaso said. Indeed, Longoria watched the pitch all the way to Jaso's mitt. It was as if he owned it. Jaso is intuitive; he knew Longoria had the fastball measured. "So I want to upset his timing and went with a curveball. And this curveball, I was, like, 'All right!'" The pitch broke thirteen inches down and away from Longoria. He never had a chance.

Hernandez, working very quickly, then brought a fastball up into the zone, and Longoria couldn't quite catch up to it. He fouled it straight back. Virtually before he could catch a breath, Hernandez threw him a better version of the first curveball, this one on the corner low and away. Longoria waved at it for strike three, then went and sat down. He missed it by six inches in two directions—he was six inches too far out ahead of the pitch's arrival, and six inches above the ball. His front foot slipped as he tried to correct his body's mistake. Longoria is a great hitter. He looked horrible. Jaso was excited.

"Longoria's at bat was when I realized he [Hernandez] had really good stuff. I knew it was going to be a fun day for me behind the plate," he said.

The key to deception, obviously, is not to let the hitter know what pitch is coming. More to the point, the key to deception is to not let the batter know what pitch is coming even as it is coming.

The pitch Hernandez threw to Longoria plummeted as if from a cliff. "See how far it dropped straight down," Jaso said, emphasizing the twelve-inch, nearly vertical descent of the pitch.

The pitch immediately before the curve had been a fastball thrown on the same plane. "The pitch that he swung at before, it was a fastball at the same exact height, so it ended up down there, but it [started] right on the same plane," Jaso said.

Jaso is talking about an important aspect of Hernandez's physical pitching form. Where a ball is thrown from—the point at which it is released from the pitcher's hand—is one of the least discussed but most important characteristics determining a pitch's deceptiveness. Almost all hitters guess at what pitch is going to be thrown. If they guess right, they have an advantage. Wrong, and they're meat.[11] One way to reduce the amount of guesswork is to study a pitcher's release points for his various pitches. If the difference is significant enough to be discernible from the batter's box, the hitter can gain an early clue as to which pitch is being thrown. Using the same data captured by the digital camera systems that track every major league pitch, clubs can track the release points of their pitchers and sort them by pitch type, inning, or whatever variable they like. Hernandez has a wide array of pitches, but almost all of them are thrown from nearly the same release point. Incredibly, in this game Hernandez threw 113 pitches, virtually every one of them from the same release point. This as much as anything makes him unreadable.*

Second baseman Ben Zobrist, a switch-hitter hitting left-handed against Hernandez, followed Longoria. Zobrist is a solid player who throughout his career has been able to play around the field on defense, and hit for a good average and, especially for a middle infielder, with good power. He was in the midst of his best year at the plate in 2012, by many measures one of the best hitters in the league. Hernandez treated him cautiously. He threw a first-pitch fastball at the bottom of the strike zone, as good a pitch as you can make, and the umpire, Rob Drake, called it a ball. Hernandez, miffed, threw the same pitch a bit lower, for ball two, then missed with a good slider that Zobrist was able to restrain himself from swinging

---

*There are more obvious ways to inform a hitter what pitch is about to be thrown. Pitchers sometimes develop tells, small behaviors that tip off the hitter. Babe Ruth, in the sterling pitching career that preceded his fame as a slugger, was said to stick his tongue out slightly when throwing a curveball. Teams today are constantly on the watch for anything similar. Trying to maintain a single release point is a relatively modern phenomenon. In the past, many pitchers threw from a wide variety of release points. By doing so, they changed the variety of pitches they could throw. What they gave up in deception, they gained by multiplying the number of weapons in their arsenals.

at. That made the count 3-0, Hernandez's first three-ball count of the game. Zobrist took a fastball down the middle for a strike, then swung at another hittable fastball and hit a routine ground ball to second. On a lot of days, hitters would feel fortunate to get one or maybe two good pitches to hit from Hernandez in an entire game. Zobrist had just two and did nothing with either.

The first baseman Carlos Pena followed, and did Hernandez another favor—swinging at a first-pitch fastball on the outer half and hitting a routine fly ball to left center for the third out. Hernandez had thrown just seventeen pitches through two. One of the changes in hitting that has occurred in recent years is in what has been called the discipline of hitters. A key predictor in having success as a major league hitter is the ability to walk coupled with an ability to avoid strikeouts. It's the reverse of the pitching metric to keep the number of walks low and strikeouts high. Because of this, hitters are reluctant to swing even at strikes early in an at bat, an approach that the New York Yankee teams of the 1990s popularized. It has two primary effects—it causes the pitcher to throw more pitches, wearing him out, and it gives the hitter a chance to see and thus measure more pitches. When teams face a pitcher as good as Hernandez, they often take a lot of pitches early in the game, in an attempt to wear him down and get him out of the game. The Rays were doing the opposite.

Hernandez's teammates got a runner as far as second in their half of the second inning, but a fly ball to left center ended the small threat. No score after two.

3

THE SPITBALL

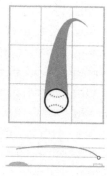

INNOCENCE

Cascade, Iowa, my hometown, had no library, no movie theater, no football field. We hunted rabbits and squirrels. We swam naked in the river, wrapped in mud, and smoked the fish we caught beside it. At night, we stole grapes and apples from neighbors' yards, threw fresh-off-the-vine stolen tomatoes at the big Peterbilt tractor-trailers as they blared through town on U.S. 151. The town has since added a stoplight. In those years, the trucks barely slowed down, much less stopped. We chased fireflies and, lest this seem too romantic, killed the little suckers, too, and smeared their lights on our foreheads like war paint. We also played baseball.

Cascade is and has been a baseball town. As kids, we played four or five hours a day. And not just the boys. My sister, Kathy, was the best hitter in town until she realized she was a girl and retired to more girly things, like algebra and French, at which she was also the best. Banners strung along Main Street sport a sort of informal city coat of arms. There are on the flags depictions of three things—a bridge over the waterfall the town name commemorates, a pair of cornstalks—no explanation necessary; this is Iowa—and a baseball. When the town team has a game scheduled that evening, banners are posted along Main Street announcing "Baseball Tonight."

In trying to think of how to describe that time and place, I'm often reduced to what seems like cliché. Iowa is the most settled place of any size on earth. There is not a single acre of wilderness in the entire state, and a remarkable 89 percent of its land is under active cultivation; even given its modest size, in most years more land is harvested here than in any other state in the union. It is almost literally a farm state. Yet, according to census data, the state has more people with master's degrees than tractors, and very few— about 6 percent—of its 2.9 million people actually live on farms. Nor do they live in cities. By coastal standards, there are no big cities—Des Moines, the capital, has a quarter-million people, and only one other city has even half that amount. But there are hundreds of little towns, spread more or less evenly, like frosting across a single-layer cake, covering the place end to end, with not many swirls or dips.

Until the post–World War II dominion of electronic media, these little towns inhabited their own worlds and were as close to self-sufficient as you could get and still claim to belong to twentieth-century America. Some towns were little more than a church, a crossroads, and a filling station. Most were more substantial, with local schools, newspapers, libraries, grocers, and granaries. Cascade, with a dam on the Maquoketa River, had its own electric power plant, its own telephone company, even at one time its own opera house.

All the towns, no matter their size, had baseball teams. Many of these clubs started around the turn of the century, often mowing pastures into playing fields. Some of the old fields are still in use. One, in the hamlet of Pleasant Grove, had a creek instead of a fence around the outfield, giving the baseball term "diving catch" an almost literal meaning. Other fields were so topographically challenged that when the catcher crouched behind home plate he'd lose sight of his outfielders.

That Iowa is worlds away from where I am now, from where any of us are now—the last innocent place in a world without innocence. In recollection, we tend to regard a place like Cascade as a pure place in a world gone to hell in a hand basket.

Of course, it *was* innocent, and just as obviously not. My hometown was a bastion of illiberality. My Irish father and German mother, both Roman Catholic, were considered a mixed marriage. Each family frowned on the other. Women didn't work or, if they knew what was good for them, complain. If they did work, it was the equivalent of wearing a scarlet "P." "We're poor," it shouted, and everyone assumed the family was a small step away from the county home. My father for years forbade my mother, one of the most resourceful and talented people I've ever met, from working, for precisely this reason, until my mother's persistence and the family's apparently infinite needs overwhelmed his pride.

Town folk could be nosy, spiteful, and downright mean. Which is to say, they were human. We knew less than nothing about people who weren't white. Black people were routinely derided as lazy good-for-nothings by whites who had never met a single example. Latinos were Trini Lopez on the radio. Asians didn't exist except in tales of World War II.

But the place, if not innocent, dwelled in the last light of an era when innocence was at least thought possible. We helped one another as we were able. In the winter, at my father's insistence, I shoveled sidewalks around my whole damned block so the old people who lived there could walk to church. When they tried to pay me, my father insisted I return the money, even though we had little to spare and I had none at all. We butchered our own chickens on occasion. It's true, by the way, what they say about chickens with their heads cut off—they run wild.

Not having much money meant my father didn't carry much of it around with him, not even much change. When he emptied his pocket on top of the television at night, it didn't make a very formidable pile.* This was apparently

---

* Curiously, one of his older brothers, Loras, appeared to carry his entire net worth with him at all times. Sometimes that meant a huge roll of bills in his pocket; sometimes the pocket was empty. But Loras left home for Chicago and who knows what fate. He got shot in a bar once, joined the Marines,

not the practice at St. Martin's Church. In summer, our parish priest would ask me to come to the church to serve as altar boy for visiting priests. After one of these Masses, the priest dug into his pocket and handed me a mountain of change—several dollars' worth, at least.* Not knowing what to do with it, and fearful of taking it home, where it would be confiscated and returned, or sent back to church and deposited in the collection box on Sunday, I found my younger brother, Denny, and we walked downtown— not a huge jaunt—to a café, where we each ordered a massive chocolate milk shake—something neither of us had ever had†—solely to get rid of the money. As it happened, the shakes—served to the table in large metal cylinders not at all unlike martini shakers, with which I would later become overly familiar, then poured into cone-shaped drinking cups—were too much for us. We couldn't begin to finish them and regretfully left the restaurant with half of each shake untouched. We had started walking toward home, past Rexall Drugs and the "Baseball Tonight" banner, but were not more than a couple storefronts down the

and trained racehorses later in life. He also owned a restaurant and bar, a fruit stand, and a Western clothing store. Horses are trained at dawn. Bars close after midnight. I worked for Loras for a while. The only time I ever observed him sleeping was when he drove us home after closing the bar. At every stoplight, and often in between, he'd doze off. Every once in a while, he'd smack himself in the face to wake up. These were not little love taps: he'd slug himself. Loras was weird. No wonder he left Cascade.

* Makes one wonder if he was robbing the collection box.

† We weren't poor but we were many—seven kids, two parents—and did not have a lot of money. We slept two or three to a room and had one bathroom for everyone. When the family went to the local drive-in, if you wanted a root beer float you had to negotiate with a sibling: one of you could get root beer and the other ice cream, so you could combine them. No single child could order both. We did not regard this as deprivation, then or now.

street when, in front of the Cascade Hotel, we simultane-
ously burped, paused, looked at one another, and without a word about-faced back into the café to finish our
business.

Since then, I've been around the world a couple times
in both directions. I've been proud and I've been lost. I've
done things I shouldn't have, often for very poor reasons,
on four of the seven continents. I've got my sights on the
other three.

I've had my life threatened—not often, but I'm soon
going to need the fingers of two hands to count the
occasions. I've made more money than my parents ever
counted and am poor in almost every important way you
can imagine. I don't have any money, either. Yet I'm fairly
certain my youngest daughter has more shoes in her closet
right now than I've owned in my entire life. This would
be an admittedly difficult claim to prove. First, you'd have
to be able to get into the closet

The shoe thing has taken me some time to get used
to. We were a minimum-shoe household. I actually wore
a pair of boots my dad had brought home from World
War II. Yes, I had shoes older than me. A pair of school
shoes bought in September had best last till June. I pol-
ished my cordovan penny loafers more often my freshman
year in high school than I have all of my shoes since.

My father used to get mad at me if my feet grew. Yet the
same guy took me to a sporting goods store in Dubuque,
the county seat and our nearest town of any size, where
we stared in awe at a pair of bright white baseball cleats,
years before Charlie Finley's fancy rainbow A's, who in the
late 1960s were the first major league team to wear white

shoes. I was at the time using a baseball glove handed down not just from my father but from an earlier era. It was a three-fingered model of the sort that infielders once used; your ring finger and middle finger shared a compartment. Why, I've no idea. I kept that glove alive for years, borrowing my mother's crochet hooks to restring it twice. The leather eventually just disintegrated. The first new glove I ever had was one that had been mailed to a nonexistent address in town that somehow never got returned to sender. My father, a postal worker, brought it home.

The white cleats, the salesman said, were kangaroo skin. Kangaroo? Seriously? Who among us had ever seen a kangaroo? My father had been for a long time the general manager of our local semipro team and had purchased the team's basic baseball supplies—balls, bats, bases, rosin bags—at the store. He knew the salesman and trusted him. I wore the white cleats home. At $19.99, they were the most expensive shoes I had ever owned.

I guess the lesson—other than the obvious notion not to ever, *ever,* trust a salesman—was that, confronted by baseball, innocence yields. Even our Iowa innocence. We would, apparently, do anything for baseball, evidently including stealing items out of the U.S. mail and subsidizing the death of albino kangaroos.

RED FABER

In the great Chocolate Milk Shake Caper recounted above, that hotel my brother and I were passing as we burped was built by the Faber family, local stalwarts late in the nineteenth and early in the twentieth century. They had a son named Urban, which was common as both a first and a last name locally. Common, perhaps, but not much spoken; Urban of course had a nickname. He was known as Red. Urban, unironically, was born on a farm outside town, moved in for a few years after his family built the hotel, then left to attend boarding schools in Dubuque. That brief local residence was enough to get his name now affixed to signs on the U.S. 151 bypass heading into town. Cascade: "Home of Red Faber." You very well may never have heard of Red Faber, but he's in the baseball Hall of Fame.

He played ball at school, but not particularly well. He bloomed a couple years later at a small college in Dubuque. From there he went to the old Three-I League, where he threw a perfect game, with only one ball actually reaching the outfield. This attracted the attention of a major league team, the Pittsburgh Pirates, which signed him to a contract, then never put him on the field before assigning him back to the minor leagues.[1]

Being reassigned to the Minneapolis Millers in 1911 was a turning point in Faber's career. Although gifted and as strong as a plow horse, he had done little that would recommend him at the major league level. When he was sent to Minneapolis, he appeared in only five games; he was injured for the entire time he was with the Millers. At the request of the Millers' management, Pittsburgh shipped Faber on to Pueblo, Colorado, a team in the Western League. Little wonder—in twenty-four and a third innings, he gave up thirty-three hits, ten walks, and nineteen runs.

But that brief stopover in Minnesota changed Faber's career. While recuperating from his injuries in the Millers' bullpen, he met an undistinguished career minor leaguer named Harry Peaster. Peaster taught Faber how to throw a spitball. Faber, like nearly every pitcher, fooled around with different pitches all the time and had experimented with the spitter, which was then a popular pitch, although to little good effect. This time the pitch took, perhaps because he was injured; to protect his arm, he threw it side-armed and at less than full velocity.

In the waves of experimentation that had followed the liberalization of pitching rules in the nineteenth century, one of the largest ripples was the practice of physically defacing or altering the surfaces of baseballs. Pitchers lathered tobacco, spit, sweat, mud, tar, oil, shoe polish, and just about anything else they could find onto balls before they delivered them. According to Bill James: "People were spitting on the ball, licking the ball, sticking as much of the ball in their mouths as was physically possible, dropping the ball in the mud, scratching it, stepping on it with spikes . . . really making a mockery of the game, plus it was frankly disgusting."[2]

The application of a foreign substance to a baseball causes disturbances in the airflow around the ball when it is thrown; the disturbance alters the spin of the ball, often in erratic ways. The ball might break sideways, or down, or even sail above its expected trajectory. Usually, though, the action of a spitball is very much like the action of a modern-day split-fingered fastball—coming straight to the plate with little movement, then diving at the very end.

Pitchers had discovered this in the first years of the game, and in the early decades of the twentieth century doctored baseballs were an integral part of the game. There is no generally accepted evidence on who first came up with the pitch.

Faber regained his winning form at Pueblo with, a local sportswriter claimed, "an assortment of curves and shoots that can't be excelled."[3] He continued to work on his spitter, and by the end of that summer had regained much of his strength. Late in the season, he threw both ends of a doubleheader and closed the year with a four-hitter. Though he regained his fastball, he realized that he should throw the spitter, with less than maximum effort, for the best result.

"A spitter has to be thrown moderately fast and the ball slips away from under the two front fingers of the pitching hand and sails up to the batter rotating very slowly," he said.

Then it breaks down and to one side. What is there unnatural about that or hard on the arm? I have been using a spit ball for some years and I have never been able to discover. They say it is unsanitary. Well I won't argue about that.

I never wet the ball but merely the ends of the first two fingers on my right hand. The whole theory of the spit ball is to let the ball slide away from a smooth surface. Wetting the fingers gives this smooth surface. By the time the ball has traveled through the air, met the bat and been driven to some infielder it is perfectly dry. No infielder needs to make an error on such a ball. Of course, I can't say that some spitball pitchers haven't misused the privilege. But they didn't need to and that disposes of the myth that the spitter causes a lot of errors by infielders. It may have done so, but it didn't need to, properly handled. A spit ball pitcher always chews something. It's an odd thing, but I have had to experiment with things to chew. Some spit ball pitchers use slippery elm. Slippery elm doesn't work with me. It's too slippery and I can't control the ball. I have tried chewing gum. But that wasn't quite slippery enough. So I have had to fall back on the good old custom, now much abused, of chewing tobacco. Tobacco juice fills the bill. And I don't chew it because I like it either. In fact, I never chew except when I am pitching. But it seems to be an indispensable part of my business like a mason's trowel or a carpenter's hammer.[4]

Faber came to the major leagues in the middle of what is called the dead-ball era. In its earliest days, baseball was a high-scoring affair. As pitchers became more sophisticated in the early days of the twentieth century, the number of runs scored declined steeply. With pitchers aided by their new pitches, including the practice of defacing balls, and by a batting approach that favored scoring single runs at a time, the average number of runs declined to less than four per game. The nadir was reached in 1908, when the average dropped to 3.38 runs. A new, more lively ball was introduced, and hitters began taking a more aggressive approach at the plate. Unsafe, unsavory, or simply unfair, the spitball was finally sentenced to death prior to the 1920 season. Another new rule called for the replacement of balls that had become dirty or defaced. Not long after, and all of sudden, an erstwhile pitcher named Babe Ruth was hitting fifty home runs a year.[5] The game changed dramatically. Home runs increased by two-thirds during this new live-ball era, which lasted until 1947, when the next great change in the game occurred. It had nothing to do with equipment, but with the players. Jackie Robinson broke the color barrier.

Faber was one of the few pitchers to make a successful transition from the dead-ball era to the new homer-happy approach. He was one of seventeen players who were recognized as spitball specialists and exempted from the new rule; they were allowed to continue throwing the pitch for as long as their careers lasted. Faber pitched into his mid-forties, finally retiring in 1933. He won 254 games, a place in the Hall of Fame, and that sign on the outskirts of Cascade.

Faber was the second to last of the legal spitballers. Burleigh Grimes outlasted him by a year, retiring in 1934. That did not, of course, mean there were no more spitballs. The spitter flourished as an illegal pitch from the time it was banned up to today, despite the scrutiny of high-definition cameras that capture every eyeblink and muscle twitch on the field. If a pitcher wants to cheat, and isn't blatant about it, there is very little anyone is going to do to stop him.

The most notorious spitball pitchers used their reputations to their advantage. Preacher Roe, who had great success mainly with the Brooklyn Dodgers in the late 1940s and early '50s, made the spitball his go-to pitch after an injury diminished his fastball. He had a well-established routine when preparing to throw the spitter, bringing his hands up to his cap and spitting onto them, then transferring the spit to his belt and finally his fingers. When hitters learned what he was doing, he would throw a fastball off the same routine, using the threat of the spitter as effectively as the spitter itself.[6]

Roe admitted his use of the spitter only after he retired. A generation later, Gaylord Perry, after a decade of suspicions, inspections, and denials, and barely halfway through a long career, wrote a memoir called *Me and the Spitter: An Autobiographical Confession.* And then immediately went back to denying he had ever done anything untoward. The question of whether he did or didn't worked so well to his advantage that he became the winningest spitballer in history. Let me repeat: they're all bastards, you know.

TOP OF THE THIRD

It was a day game after a night game, so there were some automatic subs in the game. In particular, catchers almost never catch night/day back-to-backs, and the Rays played their backup, Jose Lobaton, a right-handed hitter. Lobaton isn't a good hitter. He hits for a low average with very little power—a bad combination. Hernandez disrespectfully threw him a fastball over the heart of the plate—a little up, but right down the chute. Lobaton respectfully popped it into shallow right for the first out.

Elliot Johnson, another nonregular, got the same treatment—a piped fastball, which he took for a strike. Bad move: it was the only hittable pitch he got. Hernandez followed with a very Kingly curveball,* an old-fashioned yellow hammer that Johnson swung over the top of. It was a Koufax pitch: Johnson had genuinely no chance to hit it. Hernandez then threw a sinking fastball that darted so far inside it nearly hit Johnson in the foot. He followed with a changeup that was fouled off, and another Koufax roll-off-the-table curve that Johnson swung at and missed, somewhat pathetically.

The next hitter was the third baseman, Sean Rodriguez, a developing young right-handed hitter with surprising power for a utility infielder. He had hit barely .200 lifetime against Hernandez. Jaso signaled fastball. Hernandez threw it on the low-outside corner. Rodriguez lofted a lazy fly to left for the third out. Again, the Rays were doing Hernandez the favor of swinging early and often, lightening his workload and ensuring he was going to be around until late in the game.

The Mariners scrounged out a run in their half of the inning. The light-hitting shortstop, Brendan Ryan, hit a solid line-drive single to left to lead off. After two outs,

---

*Had the conversation been about baseball rather than hamburgers, it's what John Travolta might have said to Samuel L. Jackson in *Pulp Fiction:* You know what they call a curveball in Seattle? A Royale.

Ryan, not a noted thief, stole second, and the rookie designated hitter, Jesus Montero, lined a 2-0 pitch into left, scoring Ryan.

The Mariners have been one of the worst offensive teams in the history of the game for years. A one-run lead in the third would not normally be of great moment, but we take our celebrations where we can get them. With this team and Hernandez on the hill? Hey, let's play two!

4

THE SINKER

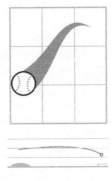

WHAT HAPPENS WHEN A PITCH IS THROWN

There are five forces that determine the path of a thrown ball. Three—direction, velocity, and spin—are determined by the pitcher, and two—gravity and atmospheric drag—are independent of his efforts. Here is a simple way to think of it:

When a man throws a baseball, it travels at whatever speed he is able to impart to it through the levers of his throwing motion. There is an upper limit, imposed by human physiology, on this speed. It appears to be something less than 110 mph, perhaps as low as 106 mph. By manipulating his grip on the ball and the motion of his wrist at release, the pitcher imparts spin to the pitch. As the ball moves through the air, the spin causes the ball to move in a certain, predictable direction.

Because of the spin, the air on one side of the ball moves faster than the other, resulting in uneven pressure on the ball, making it curve in the direction of the lower pressure. This is known as the Magnus Force.

Additionally, no matter how fast a ball is thrown, gravity pulls the ball toward the earth as it hurtles homeward. Finally, air resistance, or drag, slows the ball down.

A typical major league pitch will lose about 10 percent of its release velocity by the time it gets to the hitter. A 100 mph fastball will be traveling at about 90 mph when it reaches the vicinity of home plate.*

How does a hitter deal with this mixture of effects? One of the very coolest things the human brain can do is take a data set from its optical sensory inputs, otherwise known as the eyes, and predict what the next numbers will be in that set. It can, for example, look both ways when you're about to cross the street and judge the speed of that oncoming Lincoln Navigator with sufficient accuracy to tell you whether you have enough time to cross the street. Lucky you, huh?

The brain, at its most basic level, is a hypothesis generating machine. When it receives sensory input of an incoming object—that is, a batter sees a pitch being thrown—it projects, in an exceedingly small amount of time, the trajectory and destination of the ball. "The image that

---

*Typical pitch speed ratings are release velocity; that's where radar guns are aimed—at the ball not long after release.

hits the eye and then is processed by the brain is not in sync with the real world, but the brain is clever enough to compensate for that," said Gerrit Maus, a researcher at the University of California, Berkeley. "What we perceive doesn't necessarily have that much to do with the real world, but it is what we need to know to interact with the real world."[1]

The same brain processes are at work when you look at a train, or a car, or a left hook, or any other moving object, and you place your trust in your brain's ability to gauge the point at which these moving objects might intersect with you.

This is true of all sensory input, but is especially pronounced in the visual system. Almost all received data are discarded before they even get to the parts of the brain that might be able to act on the information. On first glance, this might seem goofy. Why throw away data your salamander ancestors worked millennia to acquire? For one thing, too much input is confusing; it's hard to analyze. And there would eventually be a capacity issue. The world is rich in data, nearly infinite. The brain, although capacious, is nowhere near infinite. Some stuff—lots of stuff, actually—has to be discarded. Otherwise, we'd never be able to navigate so nimbly the data storm we face every time we open our door and take a step out into the world.*

In the time it takes your brain to register that a baseball has been thrown at it, the baseball has already eliminated

---

* See, for example, Bilbo Baggins in *The Lord of the Rings: The Fellowship of the Ring:* "It's a dangerous business, Frodo, going out of your door. You step onto the Road, and if you don't keep your feet, there is no knowing where you might be swept off to."

a third of the distance between you and it. The hitter has to act very quickly. Robert Adair, the physicist, describes the dilemma's harsh arithmetic: "Taking the minimum effective information-processing-reaction time . . . as 300 milliseconds, we see that the batter must decide to swing when the ball has curved only about three inches—though he can redirect his swing a little over the next 50 milliseconds. Hence, he has to guess—in some sense—as to where the ball will go."[2]

Professional hitters are assisted in this by having seen thousands of pitches over their lives. They know the ball falls toward earth. Or at least some part of them knows this. As Adair says: "Some fine athletes never seem to learn to 'guess' the curveball trajectory and are not, then, found in the major leagues."[3] So the brains of professional hitters calculate the trajectory of any given pitch based on what they have learned over thousands of previous pitches—namely, that the ball drops as it travels. Balls that don't drop as much as others seem to the batter to be rising. As noted earlier, they don't rise: they sink a bit less. You will almost never hear hitters talk about a fastball falling, however. In fact, they often describe the best fastballs as rising, or hopping, at the very ends of their transit. The ball has "late action," they will say. Or it has "some giddyup." I swore my fastball hopped. It did not. Fastballs do not—cannot—hop. They don't rise. They rise relative to what the hitter expects.

Pitches move away from their projected trajectory because of spin. Where does the spin come from, and what effect does it have on the path of a pitch? Almost any

thrown object has some spin, but if the object's surface is smooth, the spin can be minimal. The key to the spin of a baseball is the stitches that bind the leather cover. If a standard baseball did not have those barely raised stitches, pitchers wouldn't be pitchers; they'd be targets. A smooth, seamless ball thrown with little or no spin will go straight until gravity and the atmosphere drag it to the ground. Or until a hitter murders it. The stitches allow a pitcher to impart spin. A ball with spin will curve according to the amount and direction of its spin.

So, for example, a four-seam fastball gripped across the seams is thrown with backspin. This results in greater air-speed over the top of the ball than underneath it. The air pressure over the top of the ball drops, and the ball rises relative to its normal trajectory. For a curveball, the spin is in the direction of the original path and a little bit to the side; so for a right-handed pitcher, it bends away from a right-handed hitter and down.

A pitcher does not have to have full—or any—understanding of the Magnus Force, not to mention any of the other underlying physics—the boundary layer, laminar flows, and so on—if he knows where to put his hands on the ball before throwing it. By holding the ball and releasing it in specific ways, you can use those seams to impart spin to the ball. If you are skilled, which all major league pitchers to varying degrees are, you use the spin to your advantage.

Because the physics of this is so unrelenting and so precise—in that the movement of the ball varies with the amount of spin, the angle of release, and the velocity of

the ball—every pitcher can develop a unique repertoire. Spin the ball differently or throw it from a slightly different angle and you will invent your own pitch.

FASTBALL COMMAND

One of the conundrums pitchers who have developed good curveballs face—in part because umps are less likely to call strikes on curveballs, and in part because breaking balls are simply much harder to hit—is that hitters, if given a choice, virtually ignore everything but fastballs. As noted, no matter how hard a pitcher throws, major league hitters who sit looking for the fastball, and get it, will punish the pitch. Take you to the moon, as James Shields says.

So, if a pitcher is supposed to "establish his fastball," and hitters are counting on him to do exactly this and donning their flight suits in preparation, what can a pitcher do? Young pitchers often just try to throw harder. They pay a high price for their ambition. Trying to throw harder invariably costs a pitcher his control. The result—consistently pitching behind in the count—is a ticket to a short career. Until they learn to spot their fastballs consistently, what can pitchers do?

One solution is to throw fastballs that don't act like fastballs—that is, fastballs that move in directions other than those of the normal four-seam rising fastball. As pitchers learned from their experiments throwing various curveballs, the spin on the ball and its movement could be affected by the placement of their fingers on the ball,

by the angle from which the ball is released, by the pressure they put on the ball with their fingers, and, last, by the snap of the wrist at release. If a pitcher wanted to get dramatic movement on a pitch, some significant amount of spin had to be applied to the ball by rolling the wrist in one direction or the other as the wrist snap occurred. That's the essential motion for throwing any pitch, to make it move.

All pitchers have unique anatomy and employ slight to large variations in pitching mechanics. This is reflected in the pitches they throw. In the earlier days of modern baseball, pitchers regarded their fastballs as nature's gift, as Bill James puts it. If the ball moved up, in, out, or in any other peculiar fashion, so much the better.

Eventually, pitchers applied the lessons learned from throwing curves to the fastball. Simply put, they learned they could make their fastballs move. James cites Curt Simmons, a left-hander who had a long and successful National League career beginning in the 1940s, as the first pitcher to throw both a rising and a sinking fastball on purpose. It has become common since. In the 1960s and '70s, Fergie Jenkins of the Cubs and Tom Seaver, mainly with the Mets, pitched their ways into the Hall of Fame with fastball variety.

Hitting is expectation and habituation. Pitching is surprise and interruption. The most common way to throw a fastball that moves contrary to expectation is to throw one that sinks.

The general method for throwing a sinking fastball is to grip the ball with the index and middle fingers aligned along the seams of the ball. Because of the grip, the pitch is often called a two-seamer. This is virtually opposite the grip for a normal fastball, the four-seamer, which is gripped across rather than along the seams. Some pitchers will also vary the pressure of their fingers on the ball, some exerting more pressure with their index fingers, others with the middle. In conjunction with how the pitch is released—some pitchers slightly pronate their wrist (turn the hand thumb down upon release)—these variations cause the ball to move laterally. Additionally, a pitcher can induce the pitch to move sideways—left or right a few inches—by altering the angle of his wrist at release.

The two-seamer and four-seamer fastballs are otherwise thrown more or less the same way and, also important, from the same release point. Pitchers can create even more movement by throwing from a lower angle—that is, more side-armed, which would cause the ball to move more horizontally—but then the deception would disappear. Hitters would soon read the lower angle as the two-seamer. The results from the change in grip are similar, but just different enough to confuse hitters. The four-seamer seems to ride up in the strike zone, and the two-seamer appears to bore down. The two-seamer drops normally, meaning it arrives at the plate five inches lower than the four-seamer. Five inches of movement is not a small distinction.

The two-seamer also moves on average an inch or two more horizontally than a four-seamer. Both pitches thrown by a right-handed pitcher veer toward a right-handed hitter and away from a left-handed hitter. A pitcher loses some speed—usually 2 to 4 mph—with the sinker but makes up for it with the greater lateral movement and often increased control. Hall of Fame right-hander Greg Maddux was an underwhelming prospect when he was advised to give up his mediocre four-seam fastball for the two-seamer. Three-hundred fifty-five wins later, it seems to have worked out okay. Maddux's ability to impart movement to low-velocity fastballs became legend. He would often throw entire games with fewer than a dozen breaking balls, sometimes two, one, or none. But everything moved, and the ball went where he wanted it to. Curt Schilling, a contemporary of Maddux and a probable Hall of Famer himself, was astonished by Maddux's command of both the ball and the situation. He tells this story:

I have watched and studied Greg Maddux for years. He is so far ahead of the field when it comes to the mental aspects of pitching that it's scary. I watched a game about 10 years ago, Maddux was pitching in SF, bases loaded, Dave Martinez hitting. 2-2 count. Maddux throws ball three, way, way outside, a fastball, then goes 3-2 and throws a picture perfect change up, not even close to the zone. Martinez swings, inning over. It stuck with me so much that the next year when I saw him I asked him about it. He remembered it, he told me on 2-2, the crowd was pumped in SF, he had great command of his changeup, he knew that 3-2 Martinez would sit FB and would be swinging and that the crowd would be even louder, the situation even more tense on the hitter as well as the runners would be going, always a nice distraction, something he wasn't sure of 2-2, so he intentionally threw ball 3 to ramp up the situation, lure Martinez into a false sense of security, then pulled the string on him.[4] When the situation intensifies, and the game is on the line, the only players that distance themselves from others and achieve are the ones that don't get "caught up" in that pressure in the wrong way, they actually hold back. Everyone else is pressing, except the guys that know their adrenalin is way kicked in, and their ability plus the extra adrenalin will do the work for them.[5]

Felix Hernandez has said that when he came into the league he had a four-seam fastball and a curveball and little else. His teammates disagree. Wiki Gonzalez, the guy who caught his second MLB start in 2005, said he called for two-seam fastballs on the first two pitches of that game. Hernandez delivered, and the pitches were moving so much Gonzalez dropped them both.[6]

The answer to the disparity between what Hernandez thinks he threw and what he actually threw probably goes back to James's natural movement argument. That is, Felix always threw a great sinking fastball; he just didn't do it on purpose. He does now. "My first year in the big leagues, I just had a fastball and a curveball," Hernandez says. "Then, in my second year, I started throwing a slider. I [added] more changeups and a sinker and now my sinker is my best pitch. I just need to locate it, and if I do, it's my best pitch. When I need to get a double play or a ground ball I throw my sinker."[7]

The data argue that he was throwing sinking fastballs as his favorite pitch by the time pitches were being measured, in 2007.[8] His sinker, or two-seamer, had by 2012 become his overwhelmingly most popular pitch selection. He will often start a game throwing his four-seam fastball for an inning or two, then settle in to his sinker. Sometimes, like Maddux, he'll never throw another four-seamer the rest of the day.

If Hernandez could consistently throw fastballs for strikes on the corners early in at bats, he'd become one of the best pitchers in baseball history. You could say the same about any pitcher. In fact, it's exactly what coaches say all the time. The located fastball remains the best pitch a pitcher can throw, simply because it's faster than other pitches and gives the hitter less time.[9] One of the things that typically happen when pitchers throw two-seamers is that they lose speed but gain command. Hernandez's control has improved gradually over his career. By the time of this game in 2012, his control was exceptional, among the best in baseball. He's thrown first-pitch strikes to about half the hitters he has faced in his career, which is well above average, and his ratio is increasing all the time.

The big problem with his pitch selection is that the sinker isn't Hernandez's best pitch, but his worst. In 2012, opposing hitters hit almost .350 against his sinker and slugged over .500. That batting line would put any hitter in the discussion for the Most Valuable Player award. Hernandez's sinker turns Willie Bloomquist, a light-hitting utility man, into Miguel Cabrera, a perennial MVP candidate.

Recent research indicates that balls low in the strike zone—and especially low and away, where a sinker to a left-handed hitter ends up—give the hitter significantly more time to see the ball. Its flight is exposed longer, and the hitter does not have to make an adjustment to reach it, as he does with a ball inside or high or both. A pitching theorist named Perry Husband calls this "effective velocity." He argues that a ball thrown low and away loses as much as 5 to 6 percent of its effective velocity. Remember, a hitter is fighting for time. A 5 mph reduction in effective speed is a gift of milliseconds to the hitter.[10]

If that's the cost of throwing sinking pitches, the benefit is keeping the ball in the park. One study found that the rate of home runs hit on low and outside pitches is nearly zero.[11] Home runs are prized more now than perhaps at any time in baseball history. Avoiding home runs is equally prized; it's widely regarded as a great strength for a pitcher.

All pitchers, as they age, lose some velocity off their fastballs. Hernandez's average speed has declined about 2 mph since 2007, when consistent, independent measurements were first available.* Some of this is intentional: pitchers realize they can do more with less effort. Part of it is the wages of time and the punishment a human arm takes for throwing a ball in a grossly unnatural fashion more than three thousand times a year.

Smart pitchers adjust their approaches, retreating from maximum-effort approaches and beginning to use more guile. They learn how to pitch. Willis, the pitching coach, says that modern hitters "can put wood on a bullet if you

---

*The decline continued through 2016, when his average fastball was down to 91 mph.

keep shooting it at them. Even as a pitching coach or a pitcher, I'm at times amazed. You look at a guy square up a ball and you go, How did you do that?

"You have to vary your sequences. It's all counts, and if a pitcher can control a count. You're not going to be perfect, but it makes things easier. We really don't have a philosophy. I always say, we have twelve pitchers; I have twelve philosophies. But one thing we do talk about is to control counts. If you can get ahead, and with the idea that even in even counts you still have the advantage, if you can maintain that throughout the course of a game, you can have a pretty good night."[12]

Bob McClure, a longtime major league pitching coach, says that sometimes losing speed can be a blessing in disguise:

It can be, because you learn how to pitch. You learn to locate better, because you have to. With higher velocity, you can get away with more mistakes. A lot of guys don't really learn how to pitch until they hurt their arm. Not that you ever want to see it happen. What you love to see is guys learn how to go hard-slow when they have their best stuff. Obviously, that happens at different times for different pitchers, and some guys get it more than others.

A starting pitcher is normally going to throw more fastballs than anything. Anywhere from 55 to 70 percent are going to be fastballs. That said, I think that more and more we're starting to see that even out to where it might be 55-45, 57-43, somewhere in there. Guys are mixing in junk more often than they were, say, 30 years ago. As a pitcher, what I'm trying to do is keep you off balance just enough, and locate my pitches. I'm trying to get ahead in the count, keep you off balance, and make pitches. That's all I'm trying to do. I don't think it's any more complicated than that.[13]

Almost all major league pitchers learn how to make the ball move. The crucial ability is to know where it is moving to. "You have to command it," Willis says. "If you can throw strikes, then you have the ability to create more movement, because the hitter is going to have to be more aggressive. Whereas, early in the count, he's going to be a little more selective and a little more movement—he's going to take it and it's going to be a ball."[14]

Hernandez has learned to do exactly this. He has consistently reduced the number of pitches he throws in the middle of the plate over his time in the majors (from 17 percent in 2007 to 13 percent in 2012, and an even better 12 percent in 2015).[15] The pitches in the middle are the pitches that get killed. Or get you killed. The fewer of them thrown, the better off the pitcher. So, as Hernandez's velocity has decreased, his control has more than compensated.

Jaso doesn't normally differentiate between types of fastball when he signals for his pitchers to throw a fastball. He just sticks a finger down, indicates location, and lets the pitcher decide how to get the ball there. "Whatever feels comfortable in his hand," Jaso says. "I figure the pitcher is smart enough on this level to know which way he wants the ball to move. If you bust him in with a fastball and we're then going to go fastball away, you probably want the fastball to be moving away from him. Some of that stuff I don't think varies from hitter to hitter. It's whatever that pitcher is doing. Just like, say we're talking about a curveball, if a hitter is a good curveball hitter I would have thrown Felix's curve ball to him three pitches in a row."

Meaning, it was that good. The more a curveball spins, the more it will break. Generally speaking, the more it breaks is one of the key components in how difficult it is to hit. The average major league curveball spins about fifteen hundred times per minute. Felix's curve up through 2012 averaged about 1,850 per minute. During this game, he threw numerous curveballs with spin rates of more than two thousand.[16]

TOP OF THE FOURTH

Baseball is a game of small differences. A hit a week, just one seeing-eye ground ball or end-of-the-bat squib, is the difference between a journeyman middle infielder and an All-Star. A fastball in on the hands is an out pitch. A fastball two inches up the bat is a birthday party for the hitter. Modern analysis is built upon finding, minimizing, or exploiting these events at the margin.

In the big leagues, every additional time a batter faces a pitcher in a single game, the calculus slides a bit toward the hitter's benefit. The differences are small, but measurable—he'll be about 3 percent more likely to reach base for each additional trip through the order.[17]

The pitcher, in consultation with his catcher and coaches, decides how to attack the offense. He determines the terms by which the contest will be conducted. If he can do what he wants—that is, actually execute exactly as he plans—he can dominate a game. This advantage diminishes as the game proceeds. This is one of the reasons why short-relief pitchers can be so dominant—they almost never face the same hitter twice in a game.

The first time through the order, the pitcher's advantage is at its utmost. The second pass, there's a good chance the pitcher has pitches he didn't show particular hitters the first time. By the time a starting pitcher faces a hitter the third time, the hitter has improved his chances by almost 6 percent.

Sam Fuld, as the Rays' leadoff hitter, was the first to face Hernandez a second time. Fuld had had an excellent at bat to start the game, hitting a long fly ball that could easily have fallen for an extra base hit. In that at bat, Felix had fed him fastballs with the sole exception of a show-me breaking ball wasted off the plate.* This at bat, he started Fuld off with a fastball on the inside corner for a strike, then threw a changeup in the middle of the plate. The location was terrible, but it was the first off-speed pitch in the strike zone Fuld had seen.

"It's one thing to be aware of it and to see it. I was out front. I didn't quite recognize what it was. Probably the best you can do is recognize it at the very last second and take it. Most of us would be happy to take it for a ball.

---

*That is, Hernandez threw an off-speed pitch intentionally out of the strike zone, just to give Fuld something else to think about.

It's the best changeup that I've ever seen," Fuld said.[18] He fouled it straight back and quickly found himself in an 0-2 hole.

"Once you get to 0-2, the idea of guessing kind of goes out the window," Fuld said. "You can anticipate what he might throw—namely, the changeup—but he stayed away from it. With two strikes, I shorten up and go in defense mode. The rest of the at bat—the approach doesn't change from 0-2 to 3-2. You battle, put the ball in play."

Hernandez squandered the 0-2 advantage by missing with three straight pitches out of the zone. None of them were close. He bounced a curveball, threw a fastball so far inside it nearly hit Fuld, and threw another fastball a foot low.*

As Fuld said, pitchers throw lots of fastballs to little guys, knowing that at worst the little guy is unlikely to hit it out of the ballpark. At 3-2, Felix went with his third straight fastball. It was a mediocre pitch on the outer half of the plate, and Fuld did exactly what he should have done—he went with the pitch, hitting a line drive to the left side. It wasn't smoked, but it was hit solidly. Unfortunately for Fuld, the Mariner third baseman, Kyle Seager, was positioned perfectly and needed to take only one step to his left to make the catch.

Here Felix was, in the fourth inning, having great stuff, but in this at bat not great control. And often that's all it

---

*To be fair, the curveball was a beauty and was intended to bounce on the ground, which it did. Felix was going for a swinging strike. Fuld started to swing at it, but somehow managed to hold up at the end. Or almost hold off. It seems clear on the video that he probably should have been called out. The next two pitches, however, were terrible.

takes to win or lose a game—one at bat. It's one of the many reasons pitching is so hard. Pitchers have to be consistently excellent. "I knew from the third or fourth inning, all of these pitches, they can't hit them," Hernandez said later.[19] He hadn't given up a base runner yet. He had this hitter completely on the defensive, but suddenly couldn't hit Elliott Bay from a ferryboat. He was lucky.

Fuld had hit twice: he drove a fastball deep into the right-center-field gap, and sliced another fastball toward the hole on the left side of the infield. He could easily have been 2-for-2, with a triple and a single and a run scored. Instead, he had done everything right and had nothing to show for it. Fuld was unlucky.

One of the great insights of modern baseball analysis dawned gradually in the late 1990s and early 2000s, when a brilliant, perpetually underemployed math adept named Bob McCracken, more widely known by his online identity, Voros, began publishing his analyses of what the variables were when a pitcher threw a ball to a hitter and the hitter hit it. McCracken concluded that pitchers appeared to have control over the number of home runs they allowed, the number of walks they issued, and the strikeouts they achieved, but everything else that happened in an at bat—that is, whether a batter got a hit or made an out—was very nearly random.[20] As he put it: "There is little if any difference among major league pitchers in their ability to prevent hits on balls hit in the field of play."[21]

The famous "hit 'em where they ain't" advice from Wee Willie Keeler appeared from McCracken's work to be nearly impossible to follow. You might hit 'em where they ain't sometimes, but not generally on purpose. Could that really be true? There must be players who are able to hit balls where fielders aren't. Not intentionally, perhaps, but as a result of their natural swings, maybe as a result of their deficiencies; there have to be guys who are adept at hitting three hoppers up the middle. The batted ball data aren't good enough—yet—to capture this, but there have to be major league hitters who are in the major leagues because they have this ability. Would you call it a skill? Certainly, there are pitchers who are revered because they own an opposite kind of odd ability; Mariano Rivera comes first to mind. But, no, McCracken said, it's a myth.

McCracken observed that the batting average on balls in play (BABIP) varied randomly among pitchers, and among a single pitcher's results over time. Absent homers, walks, and K's, he noticed that great pitchers in certain years allowed batters to reach base at well beyond the average rate for all pitchers, which computes to a batting average of about .300, and crummy pitchers were able in certain years to limit the ability of people to get on base. More to the point, an individual pitcher could have a great batting average on balls in play one year and horrible the next. Even, or sometimes it seemed especially, the best pitchers varied dramatically.

This appeared at first blush to suggest that pitchers had almost no control over their own success or failure: either you're lucky or you're not. The initial reaction to McCracken's idea from almost every baseball person who was made aware of it was that it couldn't possibly be true. Not that it was wrong, but that it couldn't even possibly be right. Yet the data were insistent. Look, how do you explain that the best pitchers with the best results seemed to have no control, from year to year, over what opposing hitters did?

What's odd about McCracken's discovery was that it wasn't really much of a discovery at all. Here's Brooklyn first baseman Jake Daubert—or his ghostwriter—in a *Baseball Magazine* article from August 1912:

> Luck in my mind plays a very important part in all batting averages. Hitting the ball hard is a skill, most generally; but hitting it safe is only partly skill mixed in with a good deal of luck. There have been batters who possessed rare judgment in placing a ball when they hit it. In fact, it used to be said of Willie Keeler that he could place a ball where he wanted to. Personally, I don't believe he could do that. I don't believe any batter who ever lived could do it.... The best of batters frequently have slumps in their batting averages and these slumps are not so much slumps in real ability as merely periods in which balls they hit, although driven hard, fail to go to safe territory.

Voros couldn't have said it better. Yet this truth remained somehow obscure. The data were freely available. The math wasn't complicated. It was barely math at all, not much beyond arithmetic. But for most of the sport's history, applying any sort of statistical analysis to baseball just wasn't much done by traditionalists. The sport did an okay job on the collecting-statistics part, but until James

and his sabermetric followers, such as McCracken, came along, almost nothing on the analysis side.

It has since been determined that certain sorts of hitters—fast guys, guys who hit the ball really hard—have BABIPs consistently above the average, and certain pitchers have consistently low BABIPs. But McCracken's basic insight—that, once a hitter swings at a pitcher's pitch and puts it in play within the park—neither the pitcher nor the hitter have much control over the outcome—has been accepted as conventional wisdom.

So why are some pitchers better than other pitchers? Because they don't walk many hitters or give up a ton of homers and they strike out a lot of batters. Conversely, hitters who walk a lot, hit homers, and don't strike out tend to be pretty good players to have on your team.*

At their introduction, these ideas seemed radical, but they actually fit in nicely with much of the game's folk wisdom. Chicks dig the long ball? Hit some. A walk's as good as a hit? Get some.

Over time, small differences—that is, advantages— accumulate. In the moment, in a particular at bat, randomness rules. You can look at Fuld's two at bats two ways: One, he was robbed. Two, he's a little guy; feed him fastballs and assume he won't hurt you.

B. J. Upton, on the other hand, was clearly uncomfortable facing Hernandez. He was 3-for-29 lifetime against him. Upton is a dead-red fastball hitter, and Felix throws a trunk-full of off-color pitches. Hernandez started Upton

---

*This was the basic premise around which Michael Lewis's excellent boo *Moneyball,* and the subsequent movie, revolved.

off in this at bat with a curveball away and a sinker in the dirt. It's 2-0, and Upton ought to be in the driver's seat. Felix threw a fastball down the middle. Upton, looking for something off-speed, couldn't catch up to it. He fouled it back. Hernandez followed with a curveball a foot outside, and Upton swung wildly at it and barely caught a piece. Seeing no reason to do otherwise, Hernandez threw another curve, this one starting at Upton's eyes and finishing at his toes. Upton walked back to the dugout.

Matt Joyce got a sinker inside for ball one, and fouled another sinker straight back; then Felix threw a perfect curveball at the bottom of the strike zone. It froze Joyce, and he took the pitch. It was called a ball, although clearly a strike—the ump, Rob Drake, simply missed it. Hernandez came back with an even better-located version of the same pitch—this one on the outside edge—and Drake called it a strike. Felix finished Joyce with a great changeup that Joyce swung over the top of.

Felix had gotten behind all three hitters in the inning and they'd yielded only a soft line drive. His off-speed stuff was devastating. He was the King.

5

THE KNUCKLEBALL

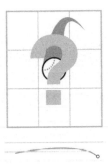

MAKING MEMORY OUT OF MUD

My father, Mac, had played for our local team, the Reds, during their glory years after World War II. This was a time of great and constant merriment such as I suspect the country has never otherwise seen. Defeating the Germans and Japanese, the last great effort the entire country was involved in, was cause for celebration on so many levels. And celebrate they did. One year, when the Reds were flush with returning veterans and led by a bruising pitcher whom the team had to pull out of the taverns on Saturday nights in order to sober him up to pitch on Sunday mornings, the Reds won twenty-nine straight games; they didn't lose until they stepped way out of their own class to challenge Davenport of the Three-I League.

When Mac quit playing, he agreed to help manage the organization. The brand of ball the Reds played in those days was closer to a nineteenth-century author's description of baseball as "a game played by eighteen persons wearing shirts and drawers" than it is to the modern major leagues. Mac's job was straightforward. Ensure that the team had enough players, and prepare Legion Field for those teams to play upon. Getting players was the easier task, although it could sometimes be complicated by the simple fact that there were thirteen taverns in a town with twelve hundred people.

Most players were locals. Occasionally, though, Mac would have to make a hundred-mile round-trip to haul a prized veteran pitcher to and from games. Why the pitcher, Sal Willenbring, couldn't drive himself I don't know. He wasn't the talkative type, and I was afraid to ask. He was built like a workhorse and pitched like one, too. After games, he would be drenched in so much sweat it looked as though he had just surfaced out of the Maquoketa River. He sat in the back of our Chevy, recouped his lost fluids with Dubuque Star beer, and smelled very much like a man who had completed a long and satisfying day of work.*

The field presented more complicated problems. East-

---

*I realize that I've just discussed two pitchers drinking. To be clear, pitchers did not drink more than other players. Other players drank plenty. It was part of why they played. In Sal's case, he just worked harder, as all pitchers do. Apart from pitchers and catchers, most waitresses work harder than baseball players, who largely just stand around during their office hours.

ern Iowa is dryland farm country. It is the westernmost farm region in the country that does not rely largely on irrigation—meaning it rains in the summer. This was helpful as a way to make things grow and potentially make farmers shut up. Note: I say "potentially."

Farmers are idiosyncratic. Many are political conservatives much prone to complaining about Big Government. More fundamentally, is there a more radical way to make a living than putting seeds in the ground, hoping it rains enough so you'll have grown something to sell four months later, knowing full well that in between spring and harvest is a murder line of lightning, hail, wind, insects, fungus, and drought? They would tell you loudly and often "no." They'd sit inside at Joe Althoff's Champion gas station tossing dice and bitch. They'd sit across the street at Biddy Dunkel's feed-and-implement store and bitch. They'd sit downtown in Jake's barbershop and bitch. Sometimes they'd throw in a little bullshit, but their main form of discourse was bitching.

Man, we town folk would think, if we could just get a good storm through here, maybe these guys would quit complaining. I didn't know it then, but farmers seldom quit complaining. Given just the three subjects that made up their entire songbook—weather, government, and their neighbors' work habits—any self-respecting farmer could sing from sunup to sundown, stopping only for the occasional hand of double-deck pinochle; or to cash his federal crop-support check en route to Hawaii for Thanksgiving.

But even world-class complainers would fall quiet in the face of an eastern Iowa August thunderstorm. Fear, not satisfaction, shut them up. *Be careful,* they must have whispered, *someone up there is listening, and they don't appear to be happy.* The fierce storms were good for corn and soybeans, not so great for baseball.

Contemporary professional ball fields are expertly engineered to drain water. A thunderstorm at five o'clock yields a dry field by game time. Our ball fields were not expertly engineered. They generally were not engineered at all, but by and large empty pastures before they became ball fields. Converting them to sporting venues mainly meant planting grass and cutting it. I doubt a single one of them ever saw a bulldozer. Some had need of it.

The Reds then played in the Prairie League. Most teams in the league had a tournament during the summer. These were sixteen-team, two-week-long affairs. As surely as the black earth around us would in the autumn produce abundance, that tournament would produce rain. The only question was how much. During our tournament, locals would look anxiously to a flagpole outside the drugstore to see if Ade Kurt was flying the "Baseball Tonight" banner.

Mac was a cross between a dreamer and a schemer. He worked at the post office, eventually becoming the local postmaster. When that became too bureaucratic— although it's hard to imagine how much bureaucracy there could possibly have been in an office the size of a two-car garage—he considered moving the family, which, in Roman Catholic fashion, was expanding at an untenable rate, to either Algeria or Australia. I don't know where he plucked those two destinations from. Maybe he had the first volume of a Time-Life series on the nations of the world. There was some sort of civil service gig he thought he could get. In any event, he never moved. Not across the street, much less the globe. Instead, he transferred to a rural mail route. He loved the countryside. Many days, he would go out after work with a dog and walk through the woods, sometimes carrying a shotgun and pretending to hunt, often just him and the dog and no firearm at all. Other times, he'd bring fishing gear and wet a line in a fishless creek. The outcome didn't matter. Being out did.

An urbanite, I wonder at times what he sought in that solitude. I like to be alone as well, but alone in a crowd, not alone with a bird dog and a bunch of squirrels. The rural route gave him time to be by himself, traipsing about the land with his schemes. He was a generally reasonable man, but on the mail route be was transformed. He raced down those gravel tracks like Mad Max in his own Iowa Thunderdome. In the winter, he gloried in blizzards that would dump so much snow on the roads that the county grading crews quit work for the nearest bar. Not Mac—he would approach a ten-foot-tall snowdrift not by slowing down, but by tromping hard on the accelerator to try to smash through the frozen white wall. He did this not out of loyalty to the "neither rain nor hail" code of carriers, but out of zest for the delightful opportunity that a storm posed. I went with him on some of these wild rides, and hitting a snowdrift at 40 mph was like being in a cinematic dream sequence—there was no noise, no external world, just you and the snow and the mail and Arthur Godfrey at a desk in Chicago on the radio.

Sometimes attacking a drift head-on worked, and the Chevy would burst through the snowbank to land clean on the relatively open road ahead. Sometimes it didn't, and the car would itself be frozen mid-drift or lose bearings and find the ditch. It didn't matter to Mac. Wait here, he would say. He'd wade through the snow to the nearest farmhouse, whose inhabitants unfailingly started up a tractor, hitched it to our car, and dragged the Chevy free. I don't think anyone ever refused. This might have been simple good neighbor behavior—he was, after all, busting his butt, not to mention his bumper, to deliver their subsidy checks so they could finish packing for Hawaii. More likely, I think they wanted to make sure the mad-as-a-hatter mailman was sent on his way as quickly as possible.

In a similar way, Mac welcomed the havoc the summer thunderstorms caused at the ballpark. He liked problems, which is not the same as saying he was great at solving them. He never lacked for an idea, and he was not a man afraid of a difficult solution. Once, I walked into the backyard and found him frying pork chops on the lid of a garbage can. What the hell? I said. He explained that the chops were freezer-burned and the dog had to be fed and he didn't want to give him raw meat. As if it were the most natural thing in the world, he had lit the trash in the can on fire and was sautéing the pork on its lid. The dog sat beside him, his tail beating the ground with excitement at having found a human who understood how the world ought to work.

Part of Mac's genius was a willingness to turn useless human beings into tools. We sometimes trimmed our evergreen hedge at home by lifting a power lawn mower and walking the length of it, my father on one side, me on the other, while the mower roared and chopped, sending remnants of the hedge in every direction. I said he embraced difficult solutions. I did not say they were effective. Or sane.

When the field got soaked in the early morning of an evening tournament doubleheader, calling the game because of wet conditions was not an option. Unless Noah crested the horizon in his ark, the field would be ready. We tried everything. We tried to bury the mud with sand and ended up with muddy sand. We poured gallons and gallons of home heating oil on top of the field and set it afire, hoping to burn off the water, but generally succeeded only in drawing up more water from beneath the surface.

Once, when the gasoline and the sand had both failed, Mac tried to rent a helicopter to fly low over the field and blow it dry. To my knowledge, helicopters had visited Cascade only twice—once to bring Santa Claus, whose team of reindeer inexplicably could not fly that winter, and another time to bring Marshal J, a regional television cartoon-show host who, in the process of putting on a sharpshooting exhibition, proceeded not so sharply to shoot himself in the foot, whereupon the helicopter hurried him back to medical care in Cedar Rapids.*

Alas, we couldn't find a helicopter to dry our field and had to pick up the rakes, order up another oil truck, and go back to work.

---

*This wasn't a completely out-of-character episode for Marshal J. He was an alcoholic who often crossed the line of good public behavior. According to Phillip J. Hutchison's "The Lost World of Marshal J: History, Memory, and Iowa's Forgotten Broadcast Legend," *Annals of Iowa* 48, no. 2 (Spring 2009), pp. 137–67 (available at: http://ir.uiowa.edu/annals-of-iowa/vol68/iss2/3), he and the cowboy actor Gabby Hayes "briefly ended up in jail in East Dubuque, Illinois, for staging a gunfight (with blanks) in the main street while both were intoxicated. . . ."

The sun caused other, equally intractable problems. When daylight saving time was initiated in the 1960s, the sun could not go down fast enough to suit ballplayers or my father. It rose behind home plate and set beyond center field. In the process of setting, it blinded hitters—not to mention the catcher, the umpire, and a good portion of the crowd. My father and his friends planted a row of poplars beyond the fence to block the sun, but, discouraged with the trees' too slow growth, they set about building a giant tarp that could be raised 60 feet up into the air to block out the last dying, blinding rays.*

Our field was built on Maquoketa River bottomland, as flat as an anvil, and just about as penetrable when dry. When it didn't rain, it seemed to never rain, and the field in those dry years would bake to bricks with a slippery topcoat of dust that would eventually lose traction and blow away, leaving only the brick behind. And Mac.

To rescue the field, he would hook to the back of our sedan—the same Chevy that ran the mail route—a two-by-twelve plank with long spikes driven through it, then place weights—me and my brothers—on the plank and race the Chevy around the diamond, breaking up the

---

*The wind eventually ruined the tarp solution, ripping the tarp to shreds. The problem persisted for decades. It was finally solved only by the collapse of the drive-in movie industry, which made available the most distinctive characteristic of the field, what locals call the Green Monster—an abandoned drive-in movie screen erected beyond center field as a hitters' backdrop and sunscreen. This saved the day. Not to be too discursive, but the death of the drive-in movie industry was also instrumental in the creation of gangsta rap music in Los Angeles in the 1980s. The two principal founding members of the group N.W.A. first began discussing formation of the group when they connected at a pop-up record stand set up at a swap meet on the grounds of an abandoned drive-in theater. See more here: http://tmcdermott.com/music/.

sunbaked earth. This was called "dragging the diamond." When Mac announced in the house that it was time to drag the diamond, the number of available drag weights mysteriously dwindled.

The sole benefit of being a weight was that after the field was worked into some form of acceptability Mac would open the beer stand—the small building that sold beer and soda during games and smelled deliciously like wet cement. Inside, we were allowed to fish cold root beers or Whistle orange sodas from the icy tanks where they were chilled. Then we would go into the basement of the adjacent American Legion Dance Hall and shower. Because we had only a bathtub at home, Mac somehow convinced us that having access to the shower was a special treat, and eating dirt was the very small cost of admission.*

The work didn't end with field prep. After the shower—Mac was right: showers are great; I still take them—we would go home for supper and return to other jobs. There was a hierarchy here. The entry level was collecting pop bottles. When you bought a bottle of Whistle or Coke or Hires at the stand at Legion Field, they didn't give you a cup, they gave you the bottle, which they then had to find a way to retrieve, since the bottles were redeemable for three cents apiece.

They hired kids to collect them. When we came into

---

* He liked dragging people behind motor vehicles. In winter, we would hitch sleds to the car's back bumper and go sailing over country roads at 20 or 30 mph. We were on the sleds. He would drive and sing Christmas carols and giggle. He once persuaded my mother to go for a ride. He maneuvered the car such that she was thrown off the sled and tumbled into a ditch. Mac exhibited entirely too much glee for the satisfaction of my mother, who did not share the joke.

the park, we would march straight over to the pop stand, get a wooden case, then head out into the crowd to search for empties. The park paid a dime for each case of empties returned. Competition was tough. Instead of vendors hawking soft drinks, we marched through the crowd calling "Pop bottles, pop bottles."

On nights when there were more freelance collectors than usual, this kind of mass marketing was insufficient. You couldn't afford to wait for a bottle to be emptied. "Can I have your bottle when you're done with it?" we would ask of people who had barely begun to drink.

It wasn't until I started going to other parks that I understood how unusual our world was. In major league parks, nobody collected the empties. Even more astounding, nobody collected foul balls. The fans didn't always return them at our place, either. Sometimes they had to be persuaded.

Ball chaser was the next job up from bottle collector. It ought to have been called "ball fighter." Every foul ball that escaped the playing field had to be retrieved. We ball chasers patrolled the park and took flight at every crack of the bat, alert for a foul coming our way. Out-of-town kids invariably tried to keep the balls if they got them, and this was not allowed. I chased kids halfway across town and fought when fights were inevitable. I was not much of a fighter—wiry, but small—and my main tactic was speed. I ran and dived to fetch balls under bleachers and cars in the parking lot. This paid fifty cents a night.

After I got too old and slow and smart to chase fouls—kind of like the evolution of a hitter—I spent a season as head ball boy. I gathered the balls from the chasers and retrieved everything inside the fence. I rubbed cornmeal on the dew-wetted balls to dry them before delivering them to Red Jennings, the umpire, and back into play. This paid seventy-five cents, and there were no fights. Even if he was calling a lousy game, I knew better than to fight with Red. He'd toss me in a heartbeat.

The highlight of my ball boy career was a visit to Legion Field by Satchel Paige and his barnstorming team to play an exhibition against the local nine. This must have been about 1962, a decade after Paige had officially retired. He would have been fifty-six by then and still threw well. I knew Paige was a legend, but didn't fully appreciate the regard in which he was held. That he was one of the two or three best pitchers who ever lived was an idea whose time had not quite arrived. All I knew was, he was older than my father and skinnier than a cornstalk, with more wrinkles than a road map.

The exhibition was interrupted by a power outage that left the field half lit. You could see what was going on, but just barely. When the power went out, there was a strong sentiment to quit for the night, but Paige insisted on fulfilling his contract. So the game went on. If you thought he was tough to hit on Sunday afternoon, you should have seen him on Thursday night. Whew.

As the head ball boy, I sat inside the fence near the home on-deck circle. When Satch came on deck, he waved me over and asked what I was doing with the balls. I explained how I cleaned and dried the dew off them with cornmeal. He said, if it was all the same to me, he didn't want to see any more clean balls the rest of the night. Let's have some fun, he said, and winked.

After the ball boy gig, I ran the scoreboard, the operation of which consisted primarily of ducking the water balloons, dirt clods, beer cans, and various other projectiles aimed at the board throughout the course of beer-soaked doubleheaders.

KNUCKLED

Mac played baseball with us, his children, more for his entertainment than for ours. He had been a part-time catcher in his day and, like most of those who wore the tools of ignorance, he fancied himself a helluva lot smarter than the dumb clucks who were throwing him the ball—the pitchers. He used to make me take the catcher's mitt—the pudd, as it was called then—and try to catch the knuckleball he had worked on for twenty years. Needless to say, I had not spent twenty years figuring out how to catch it.

The knuckleball is the oddest pitch with the longest history in the big leagues. Other novelty pitches come and go, sometimes more than once. The eephus pitch, a gloriously incongruous, slow-rolling rainbow launched high over everyone's head and intended to return to earth somewhere in the vicinity of home plate, makes appearances in the majors every few decades, then, like a comet, disappears for another lifetime.

Other specialties have longer moments in the sun—or, more usually, under the lights—before disappearing entirely. The screwball was once a common pitch, basi-

cally a reverse curveball thrown to opposite-handed hitters. But people suspected it caused injuries to pitchers, in
large part because a couple of screwball specialists ended
up with their arms permanently warped: the crook of
their elbow faced directly into the rib cage, leaving their
hands to hang weirdly at their sides, facing backward, as
if preparing to wave at someone in the rearview mirror.

Christy Mathewson of the turn-of-the-century New
York Giants was one of the greatest pitchers in major
league history and one of the first and greatest screwball
pitchers of all time. He called his scroogie a "fadeaway"
and said he didn't throw it as much as he otherwise would
have because it hurt: "Many persons have asked me why I
do not use my 'fade-away' oftener when it is so effective,
and the only answer is that every time I throw the 'fade-
away' it takes so much out of my arm. It is a very hard
ball to deliver. Pitching it ten or twelve times in a game
kills my arm, so I save it for the pinches. Many fans do
not know what this ball really is. It is a slow curve pitched
with the motion of a fastball. But most curve balls break
away from a right-handed batter a little. The fade-away
breaks toward him."[1]

There is no aggregate of data indicating that screwballs
are any worse than any other pitch as regards a pitcher's
health. This isn't because screwballs aren't damaging; it's
because pitching is damaging. The fact that some men can
do it for decades is an underappreciated feat. Almost all
pitchers get hurt. It's become routine, not crisis, to expect
young pitchers to injure their arms. They pitch, they get
hurt, they are repaired, and they come back. A quarter of

all active MLB pitchers have had elbow surgery. Except for knuckleball pitchers, who tend to have been hurt before they become knucklers.

Here's why: For every other type of pitch, the pitcher tries to impart spin to the baseball. The spin is imparted by the way in which the pitcher manipulates the ball's seams. Most pitches are gripped so that the pitcher's fingers contact the seams, and most pitches are released by the pitcher with a snap of his wrist. The amount of contact with the seams, along with the direction and speed of the throwing motion and the snap, dictate the type and amount of break. When you watch this in slow motion, it becomes obvious how violent an action it is. The shoulder and elbow especially but also the torso are put under sudden, enormous stress by the action. Imagine doing this a hundred times in three hours, or three thousand times in a season. No wonder pitchers soak their arms in buckets of ice and swaddle them in ointment after games.

For some pitches, the spin approaches three thousand revolutions per minute. Spin correlates with movement, and the movement is correlated with the direction of the spin. Backspin causes a ball to rise, or at least to appear to. As we've mentioned, a ball with backspin falls less, so the hitter reads its trajectory as a deviation from the expected path—a rise. Sidespin causes a ball to alter its trajectory in the direction of the spin. The more spin, the more alteration, the more break. All these pitches break according to a predictable path.

The typical knuckleball is gripped with the fingertips—not the knuckles, as the name implies—in a sort of claw grip. There is usually no contact with the seams at all.

The pitch is released with as little wrist snap as possible. It is closer to being pushed out of the hand than thrown. The idea is to impart as little spin as possible, and many knuckleballs, in fact, don't complete a single revolution en route to the hitter.

What happens when a ball is thrown essentially without spin? All kinds of weird stuff. Willie Stargell described Joe Niekro's knuckleball as "a butterfly with hiccups."* "Butterfly" is an apt analogy. A well-thrown knuckleball flutters; it moves in unpredictable directions. In wind tunnel tests, knuckleballs have moved as much as two feet in one direction, then back again before crossing the plate. The physicist Robert K. Adair declares it is "simply not possible to purposefully hit the breaking knuckleball."[2]

Recall that it is the stitches on the ball that cause movement, because they interrupt the airflow around the ball as it travels. Because the knuckleball spins so slowly, the stitches' contact with the airflow is erratic, causing the movement to be erratic.[3]

Typically, a knuckler will suddenly dart down and to one side or the other; it is normally impossible to know which. Catchers have a hard time catching it, because they don't know where it's going. Bob Uecker, the former catcher and longtime broadcaster, said the best way to catch a knuckleball was "wait'll it stops rolling, then go to the backstop and pick it up." The catcher's problem goes far beyond just catching the pitch. With a normal pitch,

---

* Stargell missed his calling. Remember how he described trying to hit Koufax's curveball as trying to drink coffee with a fork. Perhaps he should have been a poet.

which is to say everything that isn't a knuckler, the catcher, by calling for a particular pitch, will call for a particular speed, a particular shape, and a particular location. With the knuckleball, he just sticks down his fingers and hopes. There is no plan, just a wish.

The knuckleball was introduced in the early part of the twentieth century. Who threw it first is open to debate, but Eddie Cicotte of the Red Sox, and later the White Sox, was the first great knuckler.* Cicotte also threw a spitter and an excellent fastball. As with other pitchers of the era who threw it, the knuckler was just one of many pitches in his repertoire. He told a sportswriter that he had developed the pitch working with a teammate, Ed Summers, when he was sent down to the minors in 1906 after a brief tryout in the big leagues with Detroit. When he came back to the majors in 1908 with the Red Sox, he quickly established himself as one of the best pitchers in the league. He used the knuckler as an off-speed pitch, a change of pace.

For decades after, the knuckleball was an established weapon used by at least some pitchers routinely and many others in occasional experiments. It never became a completely common pitch, but lots of pitchers over time threw it as part of their repertoire.

The modern notion of a knuckleball pitcher is of a guy who throws the pitch almost all the time. Some

---

*Cicotte's knuckleball was different from most of those that followed, in that he actually gripped the pitch with his knuckles. Since he was the foremost popularizer of the pitch, the name that stuck to it was descriptive of the way he threw it. Most of those who followed him realized they could attain somewhat better control by gripping the ball with their fingernails.

noted knucklers—for example, Charlie Hough and, more recently, Tim Wakefield and R. A. Dickey—threw the pitch almost exclusively. There's no clear reason why this switch occurred, but it was likely cemented by Hoyt Wilhelm, whose illustrious twenty-year career with nine teams ending in 1972 made him the first full-time knuckleball pitcher elected to the Hall of Fame.

Wilhelm started, relieved, went short and long, but however he was used he threw the knuckleball almost exclusively. He induced nightmares in both hitters and catchers. One of his Baltimore Oriole catchers, Gus Triandos, once said, "Heaven is a place where no one throws a knuckleball." But he got people out, leading leagues in earned run average, establishing the save (for better and worse) as one way to measure the effectiveness of relief pitchers.

Baltimore's general manager invented the oversized catcher's mitt so that his Oriole receivers had a slightly better chance of gloving Wilhelm's pitches. It might have worked, but the team nonetheless set major league records for passed balls.

Whether because of Wilhelm or not, knuckleball pitchers who followed him used the pitch not as a two-strike surprise but as their predominant weapon. Phil Niekro, like Wilhelm a Hall of Famer, his brother Joe, Charlie Hough, Wilbur Wood, and Tom Candiotti were all knuckleball specialists. R. A. Dickey of the Toronto Blue Jays is their heir.

Very few pitchers now come up to the majors as knuckleballers. There's a tremendous bias within major league development programs in favor of pitching "stuff," as mentioned, which is defined very narrowly and usually means nothing more than that a guy throws hard.

Scouts and team executives like to say of a pitching prospect that this one is "projectable." There are doubtless subtleties included in the use of the word, but what it seems to mean mainly is that a pitcher is big and throws hard, or is big and might throw hard in the future. Or at least that he's big.

The bias toward size combines with an innate distrust of knuckleballs—the fact that it is so different from other pitches and that it can't be caught—to put the pitch and anyone who throws it on permanent probation.

Jim Bouton, a young fireballer with the New York Yankees in the 1960s, threw a knuckleball as a kid. He describes learning it in his classic book, *Ball Four:* "[Hoyt] Wilhelm was doing pretty good with the Giants at the time, and that was another reason to try it—except that my hand was so small I couldn't hold the ball with three fingers like everybody else did. I had to hold it with all five. I still do. It's kind of freaky, I guess, but as a result I throw it harder than anybody else. Anyway, it took about a week before I could get it to knuckle at all. I remember once I threw one to my brother and hit him right in the knee. He was writhing on the ground moaning, 'What a great pitch, what a great pitch.' I spent the rest of the summer trying to maim my brother."[4]

Bouton still had the knuckleball as an off-speed pitch when he broke into professional baseball, but was discouraged from using it. "Coaches don't respect it," Bouton said. "You can pitch seven good innings with a knuckleball, and as soon as you walk a guy they go, 'See, there's that damn knuckleball.' "[5]

It wasn't until he was hurt and tried to reinvent himself as a pitcher that he went back to his old knuckleball. *Ball Four* is in large part the story of how he learned to throw the pitch to professional hitters.

Nowadays, a pitcher who chooses to become a knuckleballer hasn't chosen a pitch to add to his arsenal. He's chosen something beyond an identity—a way of being. Contemporary professional athletes, more than almost everyone else, are expert at control. Giving it up is almost unthinkable. They do it only if they have no other choice. Pitching is the epitome of this: controlling the ball, the strike zone, the count, ultimately the hitter. A knuckleball is the absolute surrender of control. The reason a knuckleball is nearly impossible to hit is the same reason almost no one throws it: nobody, including the pitcher and catcher, knows where it's going.

For this reason above all others, these days almost no one goes into the knuckleball business willingly. The knuckleball is an old man's pitch, or a broken man's pitch—one or the other or both. The premier knuckleballer active today is R. A. Dickey, a former fireballer whose history of injury necessitated something had to change. "I know my arm is spent," he said when informed he had to learn to be a knuckleballer or leave behind his hope of being in the big leagues.[6]

The knuckleball for a failing pitcher is a refuge, a lottery ticket, a last chance. It is a purely existential act. As Charlie Hough put it: "Butterflies aren't bullets. You can't aim 'em—you just let them go." Or, as Camus put it about a condemned man in a prison cell—a fair approximation of a pitcher with a shot arm—the pitcher who becomes a knuckleballer opens his heart "to the benign indifference of the universe." Throw it. See where it lands.

TOP OF THE FIFTH

King Felix doesn't have a knuckleball. King Felix doesn't need a knuckleball. He has too much stuff that will land where he knew it might when he threw it. I expect him to start throwing a knuckleball when he's forty-two. He'll go 18-8 and throw 220 innings. The pitching coach, Carl Willis, has had to stop him from developing new pitches. "He can throw anything," Willis said. "He just doesn't need it."[7]

Tampa had been a very patient team in 2012: they took a lot of pitches. Not today. Through three innings, the Rays had put four first-pitch strikes into play. Felix had thrown only forty pitches through the first four innings.

As every team does against Felix, they were trying to attack early. The first two innings, Felix threw mainly hard stuff, pitching to contact. In the third, he switched up, throwing eleven breaking balls. In the fourth, he threw another nine. By then he knew he had something going: he realized he had nearly complete control, meaning he could throw any pitch on any count. Orel Hershiser, a Los Angeles Dodger right-hander, was one of the best pitchers of the late 1980s through the early 1990s. In 1988, he threw fifty-nine consecutive scoreless innings with a below-average fastball. How?

During a television broadcast long after he retired, Hershiser was asked how he had succeeded. He said, "If you can locate one pitch throughout a game, then you can compete; if you can locate two, then you will probably win the game; and if you can locate three, then you will dominate the offense."

Hernandez was dominating. He said later that as early as the third and fourth inning he was aware not only that the Rays were not making hard contact, but that "they can't even hit it." As the game went on, he said his stuff was getting better and better. "Every pitch, every count," he said.

"I was thinking of the perfect game, yeah, because I think that is every pitcher's dream. . . . It was always in my mind, the whole game. If you are going to do it, you have got to do it here," he said. "My wife—always talking about that. When Humber* threw the perfect game, she said, 'Baby, you got to get one for real.' And I was, like, 'Yeah, I need to, and just do it here at Safeco Field in front of these fans, that will make it even more special."[8]

In the fifth, Felix faced the middle third of the Rays order—Longoria, Zobrist, and Pena. He threw them only five fastballs out of sixteen pitches. Only four of the sixteen missed the plate. To say he was dialed in would be a

---

* Philip Humber, an undistinguished White Sox righty who normally couldn't get anybody out, had no-hit the M's earlier in the year, throwing a perfect game with a great deal of help from a generous strike zone.

gross understatement. Still, Longoria, after taking a ball and a strike, hit a four-seamer crisply the other way. But it found Dustin Ackley's glove at second base, and that was that. The ball was hit hard enough to reach the outfield if it had been three or four yards right or left. Bad luck. McCracken was right!

The King went 2-2 again to the next hitter, Zobrist, and should have had him struck out on a slow curve at the bottom of the zone, but Zobrist foul-tipped the ball onto Jaso's shin. "Jaso couldn't hold on," the TV announcer said. Watching it later, Jaso was irate. The ball hit him! There was nothing to hold on to. Zobrist hit another curve to left for the easy, second out.

Hernandez started Pena with a fastball down the middle but up. It was fouled back. Then Felix threw a 90 mph changeup just off the plate that Pena took. Hernandez then repeated the sequence—a fastball on the hands for another foul, and another cruel changeup at 90 mph. "How the hell does he do that?"[9] Jaso asked. Pena might have had harsher words. He stubbed it in front of the plate. Jaso grabbed it and threw Pena out at first.

Fifteen up and fifteen down.

6

THE SLIDER

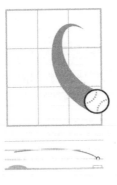

TOP OF THE SIXTH

On any given day in a Major League season, some pitcher is apt to go through four or five innings without giving up a hit. Pitchers usually say they are unaware of it that early in a game. Fans, however, can't avoid knowing. There is so much visual information thrown at them from all angles during a game that it's impossible not to know what is going on. There are scoreboards big and small on all sides of Safeco, plus television monitors tuned to the team's broadcast of the game. So everybody knew what was going on, and the park was unusually full—21,889 tickets sold, the number bolstered by a bunch of kids from summer camps—and alive for a midweek, midday game.* Hernandez is married and has two young children. His wife and kids attend almost all of his home starts, but they had just left town to go back to Venezuela for vacation. Even there in Venezuela, word reached them that Felix was throwing a perfect game. The game was picked up by local television and broadcast nationally, so his family was able to watch.

Hernandez's older brother, Moises, was a pitcher on the Mariner minor league team in Jackson, Tennessee. The Generals, as they are called, were warming up for a night game at their home park when they were told that Felix was throwing a no-hitter. The team piped the game onto the outfield scoreboard screen, and the whole team watched the final innings.

The Mariners have arranged a personal rooting section for Hernandez's fans at all of his home starts. It's called King's Court and everybody in it is given a gold placard with a giant "K" for "strikeout" emblazoned on each. The section is in the elbow of the third-base line and left-field bleachers, and fans there were starting to get rowdy.

"The whole stadium, it was pumping me up. But the King's Court, those guys are crazy," Hernandez said. "I love those guys, being always there to support me, to support the team. It's a great feeling. You're out there with two strikes. 'K! K! K!' I can hear everything."[1]

---

*More than a few people reported later that they had been listening to the game or watching it on television elsewhere and, excited by the possibility of what was happening, dropped what they were doing and hustled to Safeco.

Through five innings, the King was very good, very efficient—only fifty-five pitches, which was a bad number if you were Tampa and wanted to get Felix out of the game and get into the Mariner bullpen, which was no great shakes. At this rate, the Rays would run out of outs before Felix ran out of pitches. That said, however, Felix had given up a few well-hit balls that found gloves—Fuld in the first and fourth, and Zobrist and Longoria in the fifth.

Bronson Arroyo, a journeyman right-hander with several teams in the 2000s, once described the role of luck: "There's such a fine line between a pop-up to center field and a home run 40 feet over the wall. It's all about the precision of the bat on the ball, and because of that, there's nothing concrete about the game. You can never say, 'If I throw this breaking ball at 78 mph, on the outside corner at the knees, it won't get hit hard.' It might get hit out of the park."[2]

The patient Rays, by attacking early in hopes of getting a better pitch to hit, were instead putting the ball in play and making quick outs. They swung and missed only five times through the first five innings. Whiffs are frequently used as a quick way to judge the quality of a pitcher's stuff. Five through five was good, not great. That was about to change.

Lobaton, the catcher, was first up in the sixth. He took a sinker for a strike, then watched a curve go wide and a four-seamer miss inside for a 2-1 count. Hernandez threw another four-seamer to get back in the count, a curve that was fouled off, then a changeup that was unhittable.

The shortstop, Elliot Johnson, was the next victim.

Hernandez was picking up speed on the fastball as the game went on, touching 95 and 96 mph on the stadium radar gun. He had thrown three fastballs to Lobaton, so Johnson went up looking for heat.

He got a curveball in the dirt that he swung over the top of. The pitch looked like a belt-high fastball until it dived and hit home plate. Two changeups produced the same result. "Nobody's swinging at a ball in the dirt on purpose," he said later. "I'm making sure he doesn't beat me with the fastball. It wasn't a fastball. But he beat me. . . . It's not too much fun. All I'm trying to do is hit a ground ball into the six-hole. I understood how many changeups he was throwing. I moved to the change with two strikes. It didn't make a bit of difference. That type of movement, it literally seemed like it disappeared."[3]

The Mariner radio announcer Rick Rizzs said it "was like watching a cartoon . . . it's like a man against boys."

On TV, the Mariner play-by-play man, Dave Sims, was getting excited, too. When, after the first two strikeouts in the inning, Felix put Sean Rodriguez in an 0-2 hole, Sims shouted with glee, "How does he deign to dispose of Rodriguez?"

It took three more pitches, but when Rodriguez swung feebly and missed a slider off the plate for strike three, Sims was ready. "He's our guy. He's the King!" he screamed.

Totals for the inning were fifteen pitches, of which three were fastballs. The rest were divided among a curveball that was virtually unhittable, dropping straight down on the plate, and his changeup, which dropped as much and also moved away from the left-handed hitters. The off-speed stuff produced six whiffs, more than Felix had produced in the first five innings combined.

Through the course of the entire game, Felix shook off Jaso's pitch call just three times, according to Willis, the pitching coach. This is amazing, considering that Hernandez is a huge star and the face of the franchise, whereas Jaso was a just-picked-up spare part, a platoon catcher. The two had worked together so much that year, though, that Hernandez had complete confidence in Jaso's calls. Both guys are feel players, going for what seems right in the moment no matter what the scouting reports said. They shared an intuitive sense of how a game was going. They are also both happy little kids at heart, pretty much astonished that they are doing this for a living.

The slider that fanned Rodriguez was not a pitch Hernandez had thrown before in the inning—he had thrown only six in the whole game—and Jaso wanted to continue to mix things up. It was also what Willis has suggested. The pitch was thrown at 87 mph—about 5 or 6 mph faster than an average slider—with twice as much downward break. Rodriguez tried to check his swing, then looked prayerfully to Drake, the plate umpire, for agreement. It was not forthcoming.

"One thing we did talk about more so was, last year, he didn't use his slider very much. And it's an above-average slider. We said, hey, let's bring this pitch back into play, give them something else to think about," Willis said. "We've seen him have games this year that he's had success once he gets to two strikes throwing the fastball, because hitters, in the back of their mind, they're thinking no more fastball, I've got to bear down on this. And the fast-ball will surprise them at times. . . . In my opinion, at least in our league, he should be the most unpredictable pitcher because of his ability to throw all these pitches.

"So much of our game is mental. Because you have Felix, you have [Justin] Verlander and [CC] Sabathia, unique and elite, but you take 90 percent of the pitch-ers, there's very little that separates their ability. It's their mental toughness, their ability to focus and execute under pressure. You take so many of the pitchers in the game and you take them down to the bullpen at four in the afternoon and you go, 'Wow. This guy is lights out.' But when you've got guys at first and second and you're facing Albert Pujols, you may not be able to execute like you did at four o'clock."[4]

TOWN TEAM

The Midwest is one of the few regions of the country where semipro baseball still thrives. During the Depres-sion, thousands of teams were formed all over the country, in big cities and small. The movement peaked in popular-ity after World War II—when my father, Mac, played—but has been declining ever since. Mac's old team, the Cascade Reds, is still in business. It recently finished a sea-son with a 64-1 record. The loss was by the score of 1–0. This is baseball, remember: a sport in which the very best teams often lose four of every ten games; a sport in which so much depends on luck, where the routine out blessed by a pebble becomes a bad-hop game-winning hit, where the umpire who had seen better nights could not see the play at third.

The Reds that year won twenty-five games before their first loss, then the next thirty-nine without another. They won wild slugfests, precise pitchers' duels. They won with a dominating lineup and with banged-up substitutes. They won despite the fact that some of these boys of summer haven't been boys for a great many seasons of any temperature. The ace pitcher was thirty-eight; so was the third baseman. There were health issues beyond the usual sore arms and pulled hamstrings: the manager got a brain tumor; the big slugger got hit by a car while riding a bicycle, not a very sluggerly choice of transport; the old pitching ace caught a bat in the sternum before the season even started, hit so hard he couldn't talk for minutes, or even breathe for a while; and the team's fastest base runner suffered some sort of mysterious, unnoticed injury to a knee, so serious that by the end of the year he was being pinch-run for by a man fifteen years older (asked by the batboy what had happened, he could offer nothing more definitive than this sad explanation: "I'm not fast anymore").

Add to this the normal human afflictions—broken bones, crankcases, and love affairs, the four-year-old who fell off the couch, the car battery inexplicably gone dead, a shift change at the lumberyard, a National Guard call-up—and, finally, factoring in the always present danger that what one player referred to as the post-game "beer medicine" might be overprescribed, it's a wonder that the Reds, who had a core of only twelve players, even managed to field a team sixty-five nights, much less win on sixty-four of them.

That there was beer involved does not make this a beer league, by any stretch of the imagination. If you doubt the general seriousness of purpose of this type of baseball, ask anybody who has ever stood in to hit against the Reds' longtime pitching ace, Yipe Weber, what a happy experience that was. Weber's career-long habit of unsettling opposing batters with high fastballs somewhere in the region between their chins and their mortal souls has earned him respect from teammates and a reputation among opposing fans as a headhunter. Yipe basically throws two pitches—that fastball and a slider.

Yipe's aggressive demeanor was not a late-career affectation. He had been a hard case as long as anyone can remember. Marty Sutherland, the Reds' second baseman, grew up next door to Yipe, albeit a generation later. When Yipe would come home from college for the summer, Sutherland would bug him to come out and play a two-man pitching-hitting game popular in Cascade. Remember, this was a first-grader calling a twenty-year-old. Here's how Yipe described the results:

"I was undefeated. I'd just go over there and beat the crap out of him. No way I was gonna lose to a six-year-old."

Was Marty any good at six? I asked.

"I don't know," Yipe said, "but he sure had a temper."

Maybe I should pause here to explain the name Yipe, which rhymes with "pipe" and is so much in the long tradition of local nicknames that no one even bothers to ask where it came from. "It's one of those Cascade names," Yipe says. The town, for whatever reason—boredom? booze? long winters?—has had a zoo full of men named for animals—Squirrels, Rabbits, Moose, Gophers, and generations of Toads. And this somewhat odd habit of calling guys with normal names by some other normal name, so that a Loras would become a George, or a Kevin a Cletus.

There have been Bubbas and Curlys and Barrells, a Squinkus, and at least one Booger. This used to be common in baseball, too. The history of the game is littered with nicknames, half of them doubtless dreamed up by eager sportswriters, but enough genuine ones for us to rue their passing. From the famous—Hammerin' Hank Aaron, the Say Hey Kid, Old Hoss Radbourn, Catfish Hunter, Mudcat Grant—to the obscure—Don Ears Mossi, of whom Jim Bouton wrote, "He looked like a cab going down the street with its doors open,"[5] Harry Stinky Davis—and, of course, there was George Herman Ruth, who had so many nicknames that lots of people thought one of them, Babe, was his real name. For whatever reason, nicknames have gone the way of infield chatter in the more corporate game in the modern majors. Cascade is not corporate. There are three brothers named Ditter, Snatch, and Walleye and another pair called Dirt and Scurvy. Just in Yipe's own family there is a Tuba and a Snottsy. Yipe himself was originally (well, originally he was called Pat, but who even remembers that?) called Hippie, which was intended ironically, because he wore his hair short; it became Yippie because that was so much cooler, which became Yip because, well, Yip was sort of a nickname for Yippie; that, in any event, became Yipe because, well, who knows? It was, you know, one of those Cascade nicknames.

Yipe says he has calmed as he has aged. He very seldom hits anyone above the shoulder anymore; he has better control than that. Plus, he doesn't throw hard enough now that a well-motivated and nimble hitter could not avoid being hit if he truly sought to.

Intimidation is but one tool contemporary pitchers have taken up. In the fifty years after Candy Cummings, the curveball so thoroughly infiltrated baseball that everybody—the kid down the block, my cousin Kenny, eventually even I—threw one. It was one of the first things you learned when you indicated any desire whatsoever to pitch. Pitchers can win with just a good curve and a fastball, but they keep adding on. Yipe's basic attitude—that he'll do whatever it takes to beat anyone, including six-year-olds, to gain the slightest edge, to get an out—is shared by all serious pitchers. They will do anything. And for a long, unrestrained while, they did. The curve was merely one of the earliest and least of their deceptions. They're all bastards, you know.

THE SLIDER

The man who popularized the slider, although he never claimed to have invented it, was Bob Feller, the Iowa farm boy who took the majors by storm as a seventeen-year-old with the biggest fastball anyone could recall seeing. Bullet Bob was overwhelming when he broke into the big leagues, throwing what many believe was the first legitimate 100 mph fastball. He also had a pretty good curve. Like many others, Feller left the league during World War II to join the armed forces. When he came back after four years in the navy, he added the slider to his arsenal and credited the pitch with helping him in 1946 to one of the best seasons in MLB history.

The slider had been around for at least a decade before Feller found it, although nobody has a clear idea where it came from. Bill James credited Chief Bender with teaching the pitch to Bucky Walters in 1935. Four years later Walters used the pitch to help win the National League MVP award.

The slider is close enough to a traditional fastball that dozens if not hundreds of people must have experimented with something like it for decades. Even now, people throw what they call a slider with different grips, different arm actions, and different results.

The slider is a combination of a fastball and a curve, the half-cousin of each, and the individual variations of it lie on a continuum between the two. It looks exactly like a fastball coming out of the pitcher's hand, thrown from the same motion and the same release point, but it veers gloveside from the pitcher—to the pitcher's left from a right-hander, to the right from a left-hander. That said, there is more variability to each pitcher's slider than to any other pitch. Some sliders have a sharp, sudden break at the end, a definite point at which it is clear this is not a fastball but it's probably too late to do anything about it.

The typical slider is thrown with at least one finger, usually the middle finger, on a seam, and thrown so that the throwing hand is approaching the plate from about a forty-five-degree angle. Most pitchers incorporate a wrist snap, usually without the severity of angle used for a curveball. But some pitchers use virtually no wrist snap at all, relying on the grip and the angle to create movement.

If the slider is thrown from the same arm slot as the fastball, hitters have no way of distinguishing the two pitches until too late. The movement is normally late, not huge, but sharp. And then there are the two best sliders in MLB history, those of Steve Carlton and Randy Johnson, two rangy left-handers, whose sliders looked nothing like the typical sharp but not huge break. Both threw the pitch from a semi-sidearm or three-quarter slot, and it broke wickedly down and away from left-handed hitters. The typical swing against it from the left side was more of a wave goodbye—good to see you, I'll go sit down now. The movement in toward right-handers was so severe that they had better lift their back foot to avoid a broken toe.

That kind of slider could be the basis of a career. If you have a fastball and you know where it's going, and you can throw a slider and you know where it's going, you don't need anything else. This is against the grain of traditional baseball thinking, which holds that starting pitchers need a third pitch so that they can change their approach as they see hitters, or hitters see them, a third or fourth time in a game.

Sandy Koufax had one of the best fastballs in baseball history and a better curveball, yet worked to develop another pitch. At the height of his dominance in the middle sixties, he decided he'd be better if he could throw a slider. He started working on it on the sidelines and told teammates he would use it in play the next time the Dodgers played the Milwaukee Braves' Henry Aaron, the Braves' legendary slugger. "I'll try it on Hank, and if it works, it will work against everybody else," Koufax said.

During a day game that summer at County Stadium,

Aaron came to the plate and, sure enough, Koufax threw him the slider. Aaron hit it four hundred feet, but just foul. He turned to the Dodger catcher, John Roseboro, and asked what that pitch had been.

Slider, Roseboro said.

Aaron replied: "Tell Sandy he doesn't need that pitch."[6]

Baseball culture doesn't welcome and sometimes won't even tolerate guys who are much different from the rest of the players. Apart from his pitch selection, Carlton was as strange a guy as any whoever wore the uniform. He was aloof from both teammates and fans, never signed autographs, and went years refusing to speak with the media. He was also one of the best left-handers in history, and his slider was what elevated him.

Asked in a television interview with Roy Firestone why he had been born, Carlton answered: "To teach the world to throw a slider."

Asked another time how he threw the pitch, Carlton showed his grip—pretty typical—and said, "I hold it like this and I throw the shit out of it."[7] Not perhaps as technical as one might like, but for the taciturn Carlton this was the equivalent of a textbook. What made Carlton's slider great was his exceptional control. He threw it without the late wrist break, and the consistency he derived from the simpler motion made him almost unhittable. Keith Hernandez, an All-Star first baseman, once said that Carlton threw him almost nothing but sliders and every one was on the corner, outside black, every time.[8]

Johnson's slider, delivered sidearm and in partnership with a fastball that touched 100 mph, was so good it had its own name—Mr. Snappy. Great name, bad description.

Johnson's slider was the greatest roundhouse breaking ball in history. It didn't snap; it knifed. For a left-handed hitter, it would start out somewhere behind his ear and finish a foot outside. It covered two, three, or four feet of horizontal space. If you hit it from either side, you had to consider it a minor miracle.

Hernandez's slider has little in common with the Johnson-Carlton sweeping Frisbee pitch. It is much more similar to the pitch Bob Gibson threw en route to a Hall of Fame career—thrown hard from the exact same arm slot as his fastball, with a shorter, sharper break than Johnson's or Carlton's. It's the sort of pitch that, unless you know it's coming, you have little hope of recognizing, and none of hitting. Gibson did okay with it, winning 251 games, including twenty-two in 1968, in what was the greatest pitching season in history. That year, he threw twenty-eight complete games and thirteen shutouts and compiled an ERA of 1.12. Every time I see those numbers, I think it has to be a mistake. It's not.*

---

*Gibson was one of the fiercest competitors ever to take the mound. In his autobiography, *Stranger to the Game* (New York: Penguin, 1996), he acknowledged his competitiveness: "It was said that I threw, basically, five pitches—fastball, slider, curve, changeup, and knockdown. I don't believe that assessment did me justice, though. I actually used about nine pitches—two different fastballs, two sliders, a curve, changeup, knockdown, brushback, and hit batsman."

7

THE SPLIT

A PITCH REINVENTED

The variety of pitches thrown in the major leagues today is much diminished from what it was thirty or forty years ago. The game, like much of modern society, has been bureaucratized, rationalized. Coaching is improved, or at least more all-encompassing. Athletes are bigger, faster, stronger, better. It's certainly a better game, but in some ways less interesting. The game has benefited from getting rid of the clearly illegal activity—nobody wants beanball wars to return. But much of the entertaining, oddball, experimental stuff has been wrung out.

Ichiro, when he came to the Mariners in 2001, was viewed as some sort of space alien. He did everything wrong in the batter's box. He slapped, jerked, chopped, and punched at pitches. He ran out of the batter's box while swinging. He scooped balls out of the dirt or drove them into it. He jabbed balls at the level of his eyes. He chipped off-speed pitches over the shortstop, tomahawked inside fastballs on eight hops to the second baseman. He almost never took a called strike. Nobody can hit like that. (Quite obviously, he could hit like that. If the years he played in Japan are included, he now has more hits in his career than any professional player ever.)* More to the point, seventy years before he broke in, every team had a guy or two or three trying to hit like that. The style has been coached out of the game. The same is true with pitching.

In their magisterial survey, *The Neyer/James Guide to Pitchers,* Bill James and Rob Neyer identify forty-seven different pitches (or names of pitches, some pitches having been described with more than one name) that have been thrown in the history of major league baseball. It's a virtual festival of idiosyncrasies—slurves, fadeaways, drops, sailers, bloopers, inshoots, foshballs. If you can imagine it, somebody sometime tried to throw it.

Some of these pitches were peculiar to one man, one team, one era; others are whack-a-moles, slinking in and out of the long, weird history of the game. The most idiosyncratic of them all was probably Gaylord Perry's puff

---

*Fans can imagine the gallantry with which Pete Rose, the former all-time leader, greeted this news.

ball, which was a normally delivered pitch, presumably a fastball, that was released along with a handful of resin surrounding the ball in a cloud. He threw it only once, at least as far as anyone other than Gaylord knew, and it was outlawed within the month. Perry told *The Sporting News:* "I figure if the resin bag is out thère, you're supposed to use it, right?"[1]

Perry was a spitball pitcher, the last genuinely notorious one, and, like a lot of other men who delved into the dark art of pitch doctoring—his favorite substance, by all accounts, was Vaseline—he never knew the point of not trying anything you might get away with. The early spitballer Eddie Cicotte, not satisfied with an excellent fastball and a dominant spitter, also invented the shine ball: he ground dirt into the ball, then rubbed it vigorously against his uniform. The shine ball looked like a fastball, but then sailed up and out at the end; it was a perfect complement to the spitter, which dived. With that combination—a good straight fastball, one that went up, and one that went down—it's a wonder Cicotte ever lost.[2]

What the elimination of radical experimentation means is that innovations in the contemporary era tend to be revisions rather than revolutions. The split-fingered fastball is a perfect example.

The splitter appeared to arise unbidden and unexpected as a dominant pitch in the 1980s. All of a sudden, a pitch no one had ever heard of was the weapon of choice for top-tier pitchers in the majors. Mike Scott, Jack Morris, Bruce Sutter, and Jack McDowell all featured splitters, Sutter to the exclusion of all else. When they were on, it seemed as if no one would ever get a hit again. The split is thrown by gripping the ball with the index and middle fingers outside the seams, then throwing the ball just like a fastball. The result is devastating. The ball comes from the same release point as a fastball and looks exactly like a fastball until it approaches the plate, when it dives to the dirt.

Bill James isn't convinced everybody who throws a splitter is throwing a splitter. In an online post on his Web site in 2012, he wrote: "A well-thrown splitter follows almost the same path as a well-thrown spitter. Since the splitter is so common now, when people see a spitball they just mostly assume it is a splitter, since it's hard to tell the difference."

Sutter, a closer for the Chicago Cubs and St. Louis Cardinals, made the pitch famous and might have been the first big leaguer to use it. But it wasn't really a new pitch. It was preceded by the forkball, which was gripped very nearly the same way and thrown exactly the same way and had been thrown in the majors for fifty years before Sutter learned the pitch. The difference between the two pitches is that the forkball is gripped more with the fingers and the splitter is gripped deeper in the hand, about where a palm ball would be held.

Right, we haven't talked about the palm ball. The split was a variation of the old palm ball, which had been around since early in the twentieth century. It was indeed gripped deep in the palm, like a split, but the middle three fingers were held off the ball. The thumb and the little finger held the ball, which was thrown just like a fastball.

What all these pitches have in common is that holding the ball deep in the hand and/or gripping it with less force than an ordinary pitch allows the pitcher to throw as hard as he can but have the ball travel at a reduced speed. These pitches are the definition of off-speed. Plus, if thrown correctly, these pitches have sufficient spin to dive at the plate. As Elliot Johnson said about swinging over King Felix's pitches, nobody wants to swing at a ball in the dirt. You just don't perceive it as being headed to the dirt when you swing.

After Sutter popularized the split in the early 1980s, it spread throughout the majors like a cool summer breeze if you were a pitcher, like a virus if you weren't. Everybody started throwing it. Roger Clemens, the premier power pitcher of the era, adopted it. Mike Scott rose from oblivion to win a Cy Young with it. Jack Morris suddenly became an ace. So did Jack McDowell. Pitching coach Roger Craig had the entire staff of the San Francisco Giants throwing it.

Then, just as suddenly, it all but disappeared. The main purveyors of the pitch still standing are Japanese imports. In their leagues at home, people throw everything—it's like the majors in the 1920s. Here? Nobody teaches it; almost nobody throws it. There is a persistent belief that it causes injuries. Again, as with the screwball, there aren't data to justify the belief. Yes, split pitchers have had injuries. And, yes, all pitchers have injuries.

Joe Maddon, currently manager of the Chicago Cubs and widely regarded as one of the innovative bright lights in the game, said he didn't want his pitchers throwing it because, well, "They'll never develop their other pitches because they'll always get guys out with that pitch."[3]

There's that, I guess. If you're too successful at something, you should stop because you might be less successful if you stop. Or something. As mentioned earlier, baseball culture is normative. We don't do things because we just don't.

TOP OF THE SEVENTH

Sam Fuld led off the seventh inning for the Rays. He was 0-for-2 and could have had two hits—luck of the draw. Everyone by now was aware Hernandez was throwing a perfect game. One of the Rays' coaches had suggested to Fuld that he think about bunting, or at least put the idea in Hernandez's mind: give him one more thing to think about. On the first pitch, Fuld squared as if to bunt. He pulled back and let the pitch go by, a 96 mph fastball on the outside corner for a strike.

It is generally frowned upon in baseball to try to break up a no-hitter by bunting. Why, I've no idea, but it is one of baseball's unwritten rules. The Major League Baseball rulebook is ninety-five pages long. The need for still more rules that didn't make the book has more to do with pride than with good sense, and not bunting to break up a no-hitter was one of them. You are, for example, supposed to quit aggressively trying to score runs when you're up by a sufficient amount. Keep in mind that no one knows what a sufficient amount is.* There is apparently no unwritten rule for that. But people seem to believe that when you're

---

*The Mariners in 2001 lost a game they had led by a dozen runs, falling 15–14 to the Cleveland Indians in extra innings. Maybe they should have kept scoring.

up five or six runs late in a ball game you should quit trying to steal bases, bunt, or carry out any other overt strategy aimed at adding another base, another base runner,
or, heaven forbid, another run or two. Of course, you can
keep trying to get hits, which is the best way to score runs
yet invented. Like many of the unwritten rules, in this
case the informal rule made no sense. It was a 1–0 game.
Tampa was in a pennant race. They were trying to win
the game. The Rays' manager at the time, Maddon, said
he felt the unwritten prohibition against bunting in a no-
hitter was "archaic. A lot of that stuff to me is ill-advised,
ill-informed, just ill. Why is bunting a non-masculine way
of getting on first base? I don't understand that."[4]

"He was in such a rhythm," Fuld said. "It wasn't like we
were down by eight runs. It wouldn't have been to break
it up. How do we get a guy on base? I wanted to just put
that in the back of his mind."[5]

The Tampa hitters were keenly aware Hernandez and
Jaso had changed their approach, going heavy with off-
speed stuff. "What stuck out was how he was throwing
the curveball and slider for strikes. I think he's always been
able to throw the changeup where he wants it. The curveball, he was throwing it for a strike early in the count and
down (and out of the zone) later. Just like you'd want to.
We were pretty helpless," Fuld said.

Big league hitters get especially perturbed when someone is making them look bad with pitches that are considered unmanly, cowardly even. Brawls have started because
a guy doesn't throw hard enough. "We're stubborn," Fuld
said. "We are a stubborn bunch, that's for sure. I'll laugh,
some guys will come back to the dugout furious at being

thrown three straight off-speed pitches, basically calling the guy a pussy."[6]

Today the coward was winning. He threw a changeup in the dirt that Fuld put a good swing on, but missed by six inches. Then Felix missed with two more changes, before jamming Fuld with a fastball for an easy roller to second. The key thing for Felix's performance was that every time he missed with a pitch—and even the best pitchers miss all the time—he missed in places where he couldn't get hurt, out of the zone and usually away.

Upton followed Fuld and got the same slider that had wiped out Rodriguez to end the sixth inning. He swung over it, then took the same pitch when Felix tried to get him to chase farther outside. It didn't matter. On the third pitch, he went after a curveball headed for the dirt and hit a four-hopper in the hole between short and third. The M's third baseman, Kyle Seager, dived toward the ball, missed it. It was the right play by Seager—third basemen are taught to go for every ball they can reach, to cut the ball off before it gets deeper into the infield—but Hernandez, watching from the mound, said later that when he saw Seager dive he thought, "Oh, no," fearing that the ball would be deflected through the infield.

Seager flopped on his belly with an empty glove, then watched helplessly as the shortstop, Brendan Ryan, turned a potential hit into an easy out by fielding the ball deep in the hole and, without a care in the world, throwing a rocket to first to kill Upton by two steps. The King had dominating stuff, but, as has been discussed, there is an unhealthy amount of randomness in every baseball game. If Seager had been positioned a foot to his left, maybe got to the ball but didn't catch it, and Ryan had no chance to make the play, that would be the end of the no-hitter. Although to say Ryan might have had no chance is to make a bolder statement than might be apparent.

Ryan is a throwback player, the ultimate no-hit, good-field middle infielder. Except, in his case, he's an unbelievably bad hitter, and an unbelievably good shortstop. The only player in history who had a long career with quite the combination of good and bad that Ryan has was Mark Belanger, shortstop for the Baltimore Orioles for seventeen years beginning in 1965. He was a key member of the great Earl Weaver teams in the early 1970s. He had a career batting average of .228 with zero power yet played in more than two thousand games. Defensive metrics are still in their earliest stages of development, but they have value, and for the things they can definitively measure at this point, Belanger is regarded as one of the best shortstops of all time. In the early 2010s, Ryan was the reincarnation of Belanger. He saved more runs than any other middle infielder; in fact, he saved more than many good hitters created with their bats. He was astonishing with the glove, and yet never looked as if he was making a great play: he was so good that the toughest chances he converted into outs looked routine.[7]

Omar Vizquel, a many times Gold Glove winner, spent the early years of his career with the Mariners, and you almost never went to a game when he didn't do something spectacular.* And he looked spectacular doing it—diving,

---

*Tell me again how it is that the Mariners produced so many great players and had so few great teams.

tumbling, sprinting, leaping, fielding ground balls with his bare hand just because he could. Ryan had none of that flash. He just put himself in the absolute right position every time. He looked like he was getting on the Number 8 bus to go to work.

By this point in the game, the Rays were starting to get frustrated. Hernandez's off-speed stuff was so dynamic it was even hard for the umpire to track. A young pitcher, new to the league, would not get strike calls on many of the breaking balls Hernandez was throwing. Neither does Hernandez normally: whether it's the catchers he throws to or the tremendous movement of his pitches, the data indicate that Hernandez gets way more strikes called balls and fewer balls called strikes than almost any pitcher in the game.[8] One theorized reason for this is that a pitcher who tends to get balls off the plate called strikes does so because he aimed there in the first place and hit his catcher's target. Watch any Felix Hernandez game; the catcher is often fighting just to catch the ball, much less frame it as a strike. Felix's ball just moves too much.

Even without the lightning bug movement of his pitches, umpires have a tough time calling pitches consistently. What they call varies according to who is pitching, who is catching, and, most egregiously, the count. The strike zone for a 3-0 pitch grows taller and wider than for an 0-2 pitch. And it grows by a lot—while the physical zone doesn't change, the zone as called by the umps grows 50 percent larger.[9] No wonder people get upset.

With two outs, Matt Joyce stepped up. Joyce has some power. This was still a one-run game, so Hernandez went away with a fastball; it was off the plate by an inch or two. The home plate umpire, Rob Drake, gave the pitch to Felix for a called strike. Maddon—yes, him again— went ballistic. He screamed so loudly from the dugout you could hear him on the television broadcast. Maddon is kind of a drama queen, forever calling attention to himself. He wears Buddy Holly eyeglasses off the field and white sunglasses on it. Which I guess means he's a genius, so he's usually allowed to yell. This time, however, Drake had heard enough. He tossed Maddon from the game, which gave Maddon the opportunity to prance around the field screaming for several minutes while Hernandez wandered around the mound trying to keep his composure. Everybody in the ballpark knew Maddon was doing anything he could to break the King's rhythm. Sometimes when play is delayed for an extended period, pitchers will throw warm-up tosses just to stay loose and in the moment. Ryan asked Felix if he was okay, if he wanted to take some pitches. Hernandez declined. "I don't care," he said.[10]

Drake listened for a while, then turned Maddon over to the crew chief, Joe West, the worst umpire in Major League Baseball and perhaps the only guy at the park who likes attention more than Maddon. He listened impassively to Maddon screech for a bit, after which Maddon evidently concluded that if not even Joe West was going to take advantage of the camera time, why should he? He retired to the clubhouse, and Felix got back on the bump.

He threw three balls in the next six pitches, to go to a full count for the first time all day and to three balls for only the third time. But then he ended the inning with a 95 mph fastball on Joyce's hands, which Joyce grounded meekly to first.

Through seven, still 1–0, still perfect.

In the dugout after the inning, Hernandez, as he often does, sat down next to Franklin Gutierrez, an outfielder who is Hernandez's best friend on the team. Felix is a chatterbox during games, less so when he's pitching, but never the silent type. He tried to talk to Gutierrez, who promptly got up and walked away. Everybody knew he was throwing a perfect game; nobody was willing to acknowledge it. Another one of those unwritten rules.

"It was strange," Hernandez said. "Nobody would talk to me. Nobody would say nothing to me. I was walking to get my water and people started moving to the other side—it was crazy."[11]

Elite athletes have elite powers of concentration. They can block out the world and focus on the task at hand. Baseball is weird in this way, as in so many others, because there is so much time to think. Between innings, between plays, between pitches. There is so much damned between-time that you can't escape the circumstances or yourself. Hernandez knew exactly what was going on, which of course was the worst possible thing to know.

8

THE CUTTER

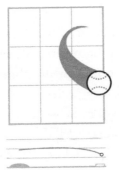

THE GOOD LIFE

Most ballplayers are aware they are playing a game and that some of them get rich in doing so. They appreciate it. Pitchers especially have it good, and big league starting pitchers have the cushiest gig of all, especially if you ignore the injury-induced career mortality rate (they get hurt a lot, and many hurt so bad they can't pitch anymore). If they survive that, they pitch only once every five or six days, depending on the schedule. In between, they exercise to keep their arms and legs strong. What that amounts to mainly is some light jogging, maybe a few sprints some afternoons in an empty stadium, and playing catch. That's it. Much of the time, they don't even have to put spikes on.

Once in each interval between starts, the pitcher will have a more structured workout in front of the pitching coach, throwing game-speed pitches in the bullpen. That's what the throwing session is called, a bullpen. The pitcher will typically throw two or three dozen pitches. Sometimes batters stand in as if to hit. They don't swing; they're just reference points. Sometimes a pitcher will work on a new pitch, but most often he just throws what he throws, at game speed.

"The first thing we do is, we try to maintain the delivery, maintain the good arm slot, maintain your release point," said Willis, the pitching coach.

"There are times maybe in your previous game you struggled with your breaking ball, so we put a little more emphasis on your breaking ball, or a little more emphasis on the changeup if that be the case. It's really a matter of maintaining all the mechanical aspects of your delivery and your release point. And if you can do those things, you should be able to command your fastball to both sides of the plate, and throw your off-speed pitches off that same release point. We use simulation hitters on occasion. There are times when a guy is, quote unquote, locked in— he may come down and throw twenty-five pitches— and, you know, that's enough. Let's don't screw it up.

"They get a feel. So many times the ball will tell you what's wrong. When you're missing up and arm-side, probably you're a little late getting the ball out of the glove, and your arm is lagging behind, and everything is lagging behind. And everything is not on time—it's all a timing issue. So many times you can show guys and you can talk to guys about it, but guys until, when they get to the big leagues they get to the point they can feel it and they can feel what's wrong. It's little keys. It's not a detailed breakdown— you find out what your key is, you need your hand in the center of the body as you separate, as opposed to maybe a guy is a little behind the center of [his] body when he separates."

So that's about it: a little bit of directed maintenance every week or so. Then it's back to playing catch and jogging.

They have lots of free time. Some become good golf- ers. They get novel haircuts, play practical jokes on one another, sit around and talk. The best baseball players turned writers have all been pitchers—Bouton, of course, but also Jim Brosnan, Pat Jordan, and now R. A. Dickey. They also tinker quite a bit. Hernandez was blessed with large hands, a very supple wrist, and often a tasteful Mohawk. The combination of the former two means he can probably throw any sort of pitch he wants, and he has changed his pitch usage over his time in the league.

The previous year, Willis said, Hernandez approached him and said, " 'I'm going to see about throwing the cut- ter.' He fooled around with it, and, you know what, I thought, 'We might have enough right now. Maybe it's a pitch we add later as you get a little older.' He has such a feel for the baseball, it's amazing the things he does and is able to do."

The cutter is another one of those pitches, like the split-finger, that have been around in various forms forever, often under different names and sometimes thrown with different techniques. Then, in the 1990s, out of seemingly nowhere, it became the prettiest girl in school, and everybody wanted to date her. Well, maybe it didn't come completely out of nowhere. There was a guy named Mariano Rivera who seemed to be having some success with it.

Rivera, who spent his entire nineteen-year career with the New York Yankees, is the best relief pitcher in history, and it's not a close call. He saved 652 games, compiled a career ERA of 2.21, was part of five World Series championship teams, and for most of his career threw the cutter four out of every five pitches. Such reliance on one pitch approaches the knuckleball specialists of an earlier time, and his pitch was no less, maybe even more, a mystery. He was a deeply religious man and at various times alluded to divine inspiration for his pitch. How else to explain a pitch that arrived apparently out of nowhere when he was playing catch with another reliever?

People have been throwing something they referred to as a cutter or cut fastball for most of a hundred years. No one happened to throw it so well. The pitch is executed by holding the ball in a basic four-seam fastball grip, but with the fingers moved to the right (for a right-hander) side of the seams rather than straight across them. Then you throw the ball as if it were a fastball. By applying pressure with the index and middle fingers, Rivera turned the pitch into an incendiary device. He did this by maintaining velocity while also inducing spin. The resulting pitch came from the same spot as a straight fastball and looked exactly like a straight fastball until just before it arrived at the plate, when it veered to his left. Not much—only a few inches—but hard and always late. A right-handed hitter would break his bat by catching the pitch on the end of the barrel. A left-handed hitter would break his bat by catching the pitch in on his hands. The bat carnage was so complete that one of the retirement gifts Rivera got from an opposing team was a rocking chair built out of busted bats. I don't know, but if it were me I might have booby-trapped the rocker, to ensure the guy would never come back and pitch again.

The cutter, again like the split, exists along a continuum of similar pitches. It is somewhere between a fastball and a slider in speed and break, all of which is horizontal. As a young pitcher, you're taught that pure horizontal break is dangerous, because you're leaving the ball on the same plane as the hitter's swing. I can testify that this is a very bad idea. Put simply, a ball that moves only horizontally gives the hitter double the chance to land wood on it. Nobody mentioned to me the possibility of divine intervention. Had I known, I might have stuck with that altar boy gig a little longer.

Rivera claimed there was a secret to his cutter, but high-speed photography seems to indicate there was no secret, just great skill. Maybe he happened upon it in a mysterious way, but there was no mystery to its effectiveness.

For a time, every pitcher in organized baseball was trying to throw Mariano's cutter. It seemed like magic—a pitch almost everyone could throw and no one could hit. Turns out, not everyone is Rivera. For one thing, others couldn't throw any pitch as hard as he threw his cutter, much less throw a cutter at that speed. And if the pitch isn't thrown expertly, the old advice about not leaving the pitch on that plane applies. If you throw the ball where the hitter is swinging—whether intentionally or not— you're in trouble.

TOP OF THE EIGHTH

Tampa's Hellickson was pitching almost as beautifully as Felix, giving up a mere five hits and the one huge, lonely run. He was facing one of the best pitchers of this generation, who was at home in front of a raucous, worshipful crowd and throwing as well as he ever had. Typically, in the late innings of a pitchers' duel, when it seems the outcome of the game could be altered on every pitch, there is a tight high hum rising from the crowd. It might go up and down with every pitch. That tension is among the best things baseball has to offer. But it was somehow absent this day. In the late innings, there was very little tension in the crowd. It was, instead, a party.

Even in a regular—that is, not a no-hitter—1–0 game, the crowd would be rising and falling with every pitch to the home-team hitters, in hopes that they could add to the slim lead. Not this day. The crowd quieted during the home half of every inning, eager to get it over with so they could get on to the real action when the M's went on defense.

Every time Felix took the mound, a raucous chant of "Let's go, Felix" shook the metal rafters. The "K" cards in the King's Court danced feverishly down the left-field line. The summer camp kids, playing hooky from camp in the upper deck and outfitted in brilliant primary-colored T-shirts, caught the excitement and added a hyper, nonsensical racket to the party atmosphere.

Still, Hellickson had kept his team in it, and the single run the Mariners had managed in the third was the only marker on the board when the Rays' cleanup hitter, Longoria, led off the top of the eighth. Realistically, he was the player most likely to get his team even with one swing of the bat. Longoria is one of the best hitters in the game generally, and especially against fastballs on the inner half of the plate. He just destroys them, hitting over .400 and slugging over .800 on such pitches. Hernandez had teased him inside once in each of his two previous at bats. He wanted no part of that this time.

Since the middle of the game, Jaso had begun upping the number of off-speed pitches. Now, toward the end, that was virtually all he was calling. This wasn't pitching backward; it was pitching in a world turned completely upside down. He went there again against Longoria. Hernandez threw back-to-back huge, breaking Gibson sliders, one for a called strike, one for a swing and a miss. Both pitches broke twice as much as a normal slider: the first from the top of the zone to the middle, the second ending up below the zone, nearly in the dirt. He then threw a 91 mph changeup way inside and low—a 91 mph changeup that broke two feet, so much break that Jaso had to lunge to catch it. It looked like a special effect, which is one of the comparisons Jaso had made earlier in the week. Catching Felix, he said, was like having the cheat codes to a video game.

Felix went back outside with a big, plunging curveball that had the shape of a diver going off the Acapulco cliffs. Longoria was badly fooled on the pitch and swung awkwardly, his butt going one way and his hands, the smarter of the extremities engaged in pursuit of the ball, reaching as far as possible in the other. He looked like he had just run off the road and was trying desperately to pull his car out of the ditch before a cop came along to ticket him. He went and sat down.

Zobrist was next. He's exactly the kind of hitter who ruins games like this. He is patient, and he uses the whole field. Plus, he hits right-handers well. Felix had thrown four straight off-speed pitches to Longoria. He threw three more to Zobrist—curve, change, curve—for a 1-2 count. He then threw a 91 mph changeup at the very bottom of the strike zone for a swinging strike three. The change broke more than half a foot. Zobrist took his strikeout and went back to the bench to sit next to Longoria.

Now the crowd throughout Safeco was standing and screaming. Rizzs, on the radio, was screaming along with them. Rizzs had religiously recited the number of hitters who had come and gone—twenty-two up, twenty-two gone—but, honoring the superstition, hadn't mentioned the perfect game. He was by now exultant.

Pena approached the plate. Jaso didn't have a great deal of concern. "He was missing the curveball by three feet," he said.[1] Hernandez showed Pena a fastball away, then threw Jaso's curve for strike one. A change for two. Then a two-seamer, fouled off. "Safeco Field is electric," Rizzs shouted.

Indeed it was. There was no anxiety here, only celebration.

Felix looked in. Took the sign for yet another off-speed pitch. Then threw the glorious curve to retire the side. That final curve broke almost two feet. It's hard to do that even in a video game. The break on the off-speed stuff was, as Fuld said, ridiculous. Hernandez was throwing Gibson sliders and Koufax curves one after another, then adding a change.

The King was on his throne.

9

THE CHANGE

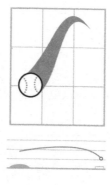

SLOW BALLS

When professional baseball began, pitchers, as we've learned, were restricted in what they could do. They couldn't throw hard. They couldn't throw crooked. They couldn't be sneaky. They were allowed to do one thing—throw the ball straight, and above all slow, so that the hitters could do what the fans paid to see them do—hit. Of course, the pitchers immediately began finding ways to do all of the things that had been forbidden to them.

There is, then, irony in the fact that the dominant pitch of the last two decades is the only pitch the old timers were allowed to throw—the slow ball. It has gone by many different names since, and nobody calls it a "slow ball" anymore. We seem to have finally standardized the name as "the changeup."

The message that a fastball sends is among the most primal things in sport: Here, buddy, see if you can hit this. Little men with big arms make bigger men weep when they throw the fastball by them. The point of the changeup is nearly the opposite; it's an invitation not a challenge: Here, have some.

Well, as Sleeping Beauty would surely tell you if she were here: Beware of gifts so freely given.

A normal changeup is indeed a change of pace from the quicker selections in a pitcher's arsenal, sometimes 10 or 15 mph slower than a pitcher's fastest pitch. It is thrown with a variety of grips—some pitchers spend years searching for the one that suits them best—but, whatever the grip, the one thing a successful changeup must do is persuade the hitter it is something other than what it is. This is accomplished mainly by making an arm motion and release as nearly identical to a fastball motion as is possible.

Hitters, like all humans, anticipate the future; most particularly, they anticipate the pitch that is coming. The human brain, with enough practice, can see a pitcher throw a ball and judge within milliseconds how hard and where that pitch is going. Sometimes the brain doesn't even need to see the ball—just watching the arm and the hand that holds the ball can be enough. Or at least that is what hitters charmingly think.

The one thing the various changeup grips have in common is that they allow the pitcher to scrub speed off the pitch without lessening the speed of the throwing motion whatsoever. He does this mainly by sacrificing direct contact with the ball, lifting this or that finger or several of them off the ball at release. Common variants include the circle change, the palm ball, the straight change, the Vulcan change, each held with a distinctive grip.

The traditional straight change required a pitcher to lift his middle fingers up off the ball, but there was fear that opposing hitters could read this and react to it. The circle change is the most common grip today. The ball is held in the middle, ring, and little fingers of the throwing hand. The index finger and thumb are placed beside the ball, nearly touching and forming a circle. The great advantage to the circle change is that, once the grip is set, no further manipulation is necessary. The ball can be thrown at a variety of speeds and retain its characteristic movement, down and away from a left-hander.

Many analysts and coaches believe the changeup has to be significantly slower than a pitcher's fastball, as much as 10 mph, in order to "have separation" from the fastball. Almost all the great changeups of the past—think Pedro Martinez, Stu Miller, Trevor Hoffman, and Jamie Moyer—earned their deception in large part by having this separation.

Jamie Moyer was the most successful, which is not to say the best, Mariner pitcher of all time. Randy Johnson was the best, and no one will argue with that. The six-foot-nine Johnson was an athletic freak with a big upper-90s mph fastball and an evil slider that was one of the best breaking balls in major league history. Once he learned how to control himself and his pitches, he obliterated hitters. And, after a late start, did it for more than a decade of sustained excellence.

Moyer was a late starter, too. Almost done as a professional baseball player before he turned thirty—the Chicago Cubs offered him a coaching job—Moyer somehow became a pitching ace who endured past his fortieth birthday, and nearly to his fiftieth.* He was almost the opposite of Johnson. He was a modest-sized guy, which is to say normal, whose fastball topped out in the mid-80s mph. That's when he was young. As he aged, so did his fastball. He won 269 games in the major leagues, 235 of those after he turned 30, including 145 with the Mariners. By the end, his fastball was averaging 79 mph. That's ridiculous.

Losing speed on his fastball was inconsequential for Moyer, since he didn't really have one. A fastball, that is. Instead, he threw one of the best changeups in major league history. A Moyer change was a classic example of salesmanship. It depended entirely upon Moyer's ability to make the hitter think he was getting the very slow fastball rather than the even slower changeup. It had a purity of deceit.

I asked him once how he had the nerve to throw Little League fastballs to major league hitters. His answer was absolutely lacking in the kind of masculine vanity so common among athletes: "I would never have had a career if it wasn't for the pride of major league hitters," he said. "They were determined to never get beat by a fastball."

---

* He finally accepted the inevitable and retired in 2014. He had sat out the previous year, recovering from elbow surgery, and still wanted to pitch in what would have been his age-fifty-one season. No one offered him a job.

Still, Moyer racked up a career of 2,441 strikeouts, many of them with that puny fastball, which sometimes froze hitters after they'd watched two or three of the dead-fish changes amble past. To be fair to the hitters, they weren't always fooled. Moyer gave up a record 522 home runs in his long career. To his credit, two-thirds of them came with the bases empty.

Felix Hernandez throws one of the oddest changeups in baseball history. Foremost, it doesn't have much of a change of speed. He uses a variation of the circle-change grip, and he throws the pitch faster than Moyer threw his fastball—in fact, faster than a lot of people throw their fastballs, and faster than every pitch he has save his fastball. "All of his pitches look just like his fastball," said Elliot Johnson. "The change is unique because he throws it so hard. Everything is exactly the same as his heater, then it drops out of the zone."[1]

When Dustin Pedroia, the All-Star Red Sox second baseman, faced Hernandez earlier in the summer of 2012, Hernandez struck him out on one changeup. It started in the other batter's box, and by the time he swung futilely at the ball, it just missed hitting him.

It is that movement rather than differing speed that gives the pitch its essential deceit. Hernandez developed the pitch after he came to the big leagues. He fiddled with it while playing catch on off days, and eventually found a grip that worked. That's something of an understatement. Year to year, Felix's change is among the most effective pitches in the major leagues.

In the last three innings of today's game, Felix threw more changeups than fastballs. That doesn't work if it's a mere slow ball, which it is not. He threw a couple change-ups that broke almost two feet down and in to right-handed hitters. That's something else you're not supposed to do, throw the change to same-handed hitters; the whole point of the pitch's movement is to take the ball out of the hitting zone for left-handed batters. Most pitchers use their curveballs or sliders against same-handed hitters and their changeups against opposite-handed hitters. Over his career, Felix has been an even-handed assassin with the pitch, throwing it as frequently to right- as to left-handers. It doesn't matter much what hand they try to hit with. They mostly don't.

"When it's on, hitters expect it and can't do anything with it," Jaso said. "They try to swing at pitches earlier in the count so they don't have to face that changeup. It can really mess with hitters' heads."[2]

Think about that for a minute—hitters swing at pitches they really don't want to swing at in order to avoid swinging at the King's change.

TOP OF THE NINTH

Almost every year, one or more no-hitters are broken up in the ninth inning. Some years, a half-dozen have been ruined that way. Even worse, thirteen perfect games have been lost with two outs in the ninth. Anything can and has happened—a solid line drive, a bad hop, a bad call, a bloop hit, a swinging bunt, an error, a nervous walk, a hitter leaning in to get hit by the pitch.

Everybody was nervous. Jesus Montero, the designated

hitter, who had driven in the game's only run, was praying with Gutierrez in the dugout. "We were so nervous, it was unbelievable," he said.

"I was sitting on the bench, shaking," Gutierrez said.

Felix's brother Moises was still watching the game on the outfield scoreboard twenty-three hundred miles to the southeast. He and his fellow Venezuelan Jose Medina were so tense they were crying.

Jaso tried to think back to how he had felt when he played in minor league championship games. Knowing that he had to slow himself down so that he could keep Felix slowed as well, he did a series of breathing exercises to calm himself.

The Safeco crowd was on its feet, chanting, "Let's go, Felix." Every time he threw a pitch, the chant would pause for a roar, an "ooh" or an "aw," then resume. There were so many cell-phone cameras held aloft, it looked like a Rolling Stones concert.

Felix was hyped, too. When he went to the mound for the last inning, he looked up at the big scoreboard in right-center field. He got the chills. "Wow," he said to himself, "now you gotta do it. These guys, these people over here, they've been great to me. Just finish it, please."[3]

He had barely been behind in the count all day. Controlling the count, in fact, was as important to his success as his dynamic stuff. So then he started all three hitters in the bottom of the ninth with balls. The first hitter was a pinch hitter, Desmond Jennings, a speedy young outfield prospect who looked as though he might develop into a minor star. Jaso called for a high breaking ball, hoping to steal a strike. He's one of the few catchers who call for curveballs up in the zone. "The high breaking ball is one of the best pitches in the game," he said. "There's a difference between a hanging breaking ball and a high breaking ball. The hitter gives up on it and has to restart."[4]

Felix overthrew it and missed up. He got back in the count with a slider down the middle: Jennings took a wild swing and missed as the ball nearly hit the dirt. Felix went ahead with another slider on the outside corner for a called strike. Jennings spoiled a third slider. He then barely caught a piece of a 95 mph fastball on the outside edge. The crowd groaned. Then Felix put a 92 mph changeup on Jennings's back foot. The pitch locked up Jennings: he swung feebly and missed for a swinging strike three. This was the pitch Pedroia had talked about. It looked like a lefty slider. Even though Jaso had been catching Felix all season, he was amazed.

Jeff Keppinger, another right-handed hitter and a good contact bat, was the second pinch hitter. He took a ball and a strike. Then he swung through another inside two-seamer that hit 95 mph on the radar gun. That is about as hard as it is humanly possible to throw a sinker. Hernandez was clearly pumped. "It was the greatest sinker I ever threw," Hernandez said. "That ball started in the middle of the plate and finished at his back."[5]

A 92 mph change induced an easy grounder to the left side. Hernandez had struck out the previous four hitters in a row. The Rays were making so little contact of any kind that a ball hit solidly in play was a bit of a shock. "I turned around quick. Brendon was there." Hernandez breathed a sigh of relief. "Okay, it's Brendon. Everything's good."[6]

That left only Sean Rodriguez between Hernandez and a perfect game. Detroit Tiger right-hander Armando Galarraga was in exactly the same position just two years before—one out from a perfect game. He induced a routine ground ball to the last hitter and a routine throw to first nipped the runner for the final out. Wait! The umpire, Jim Joyce, called him safe? It can happen. Joyce acknowledged tearfully after the game that he had blown the call. He apologized. Galarraga was gracious, telling reporters, "Nobody's perfect." Not most days, anyhow.

Back at Safeco, the crowd was loud. The King's Court was going nuts with noise and delirium. Felix missed with a fastball. He missed with a slider. Both were outside. It was only his second 2-0 count of the game. "No," he thought. "Not the last hitter! Give me the ball."[7]

Rodriguez had gone to the plate thinking he might break the unwritten rule: maybe bunt and endure the wrath that would surely follow. But when the count went to 2-0, he knew he'd get a fastball, and with it a chance to hit the ball in the gap or farther. The normal, almost mandatory pitch call in that situation would be fastball down the middle, just to get a strike.

Hernandez figured Rodriguez would be looking for a fastball and was probably prepared to swing at anything anywhere near the zone. He wanted to go off speed. Jaso had been lectured consistently when he was in the minor leagues that you don't have a choice in that count: you have to throw a fastball just to get a strike. If the hitter smacks it, you live with the results. Jaso called for a slider. Felix was surprised but pleased. "He called a great game, man," he said later.[8] The pitching coach, Carl Willis, was just surprised. "What a call," he said, his eyebrows raising slightly.[9]

Rodriguez swung over it for strike one.

"I thought it was the nastiest pitch he threw the whole game," Jaso said.

At 2-1, Jaso called for a curve. Felix threw a hump-backed beauty. Rodriguez flinched, then froze. He took the pitch for a called strike two.

Hernandez took a deep breath on the mound. He cautioned himself to stay cool: "Don't try to be too beautiful, just make a good pitch."

He looked in for the sign. Jaso signaled for the change.

"Right there with that changeup, that was the only time I thought, 'We have to throw a changeup here, because that's his pitch.' That's what everybody talks about. That's what he likes. There was no other pitch to end the game with," Jaso said. "There was no other way. If he missed with that, I was going to call it again."[10]

King Felix threw a change at 92 mph to the low-inside corner. Rodriguez couldn't pull the trigger. He took it for a called strike three.

Over the entire game, Tampa hitters swung and missed twenty-four times, nineteen times in just the last four innings. Only two of those swings were at fastballs. The remaining twenty-two were on off-speed pitches. Felix threw two fastballs and thirteen off-speed pitches in the ninth inning to finish the game.

The most effective pitch in one of the best games ever thrown was the changeup, the ancient slow ball, the oldest pitch of all, finally raised to royalty.

Felix danced on the mound, pulling one leg high and twirling. He kissed his wrists. He thrust his hands above his head. Jaso rushed the mound. The crowd roared. Sims screamed. Rizzs shouted. The game was over.

PARTS MISSING

I watched this game, as I watch almost all Mariner games now, on my computer in southern California, where I have settled. I do not shovel the neighbors' sidewalks here for no pay. For one thing, there are no sidewalks. For another, there is no snow. I'm not sure that matters. If I pick up their newspapers when they are out of town, or put away their trash cans on garbage day, I do it in memory of Mac, even if other neighbors regard me with suspicion. Which is to say, my circumstances have changed utterly. Yet I'm stuck on baseball. I really have no idea why.

When I first moved here, I discovered I could get out-of-market radio broadcasts over the Internet. I spend a lot of time sitting at a computer, and the idea of doing so with Dave Niehaus, the Mariner broadcaster, purring in my ear, was too irresistible to ignore. I signed up. Later, when televised games over the Internet became available, I signed up for that, too. I watch them on a dedicated monitor while I ostensibly work on another.

Niehaus has since gone to that big broadcast booth

in the sky, where he no doubt enjoys a grand salami on rye every now and then, but I continue, during the season, to tune in the games almost every day. By this point, my activity has moved beyond fandom. The team might not have a chance, but I'm there every day, regardless. There is no communion with other fans. There probably wasn't another Mariner fan within five miles of me that day. Watching has transcended habit into ritual, like the prayers of sinners long since fallen by the wayside.

It's odd to celebrate by yourself, so I don't. When Felix's game ended, I smiled and turned back to the work I was supposed to be doing. I received a congratulatory e-mail from Cary shortly after the game ended. That's what happens when you root for a bad team—people feel sorry for you. The mail came from her office in the wilds of Midtown Manhattan, where she had abandoned Edgar's hitting stance and become, of all things, a lawyer and a Yankee fan. There it was, though—communion. It's your daughter reaching through the ether, through the years— through the Yankees, for God's sakes—to touch you. I was as much moved by that as by the game. It's funny about children. You spend more time worrying about who they will become than appreciating who they are. That's backward, right? Shouldn't we care about them in the moment, about the people we see before us?

I have three daughters. Whatever else they received from me, and I sometimes ache at how little that seems compared with what I received from Mac, they all got my arm, which was the only thing I ever had as an athlete that was a genuine weapon. The girls could bring the heat.

Some of them—not to mention any names, Casey—had no idea where the ball was going, but they could bring it.* Casey is a White Sox fan. I say this without disapprobation. In fact, I approve wholeheartedly. It's very much like me and the Mariners. She lived in Chicago for a while and chose the distinctively uncool option of the Sox over the Cubs. The whole damn family has a problem with authority.

It's still too early to know what might happen with Lina, the youngest. She is concerned with more obviously important things—friends, Flying Lotus, her softball team, and whether the first baseman can handle her heat when it arrives from shortstop—to have even considered fandom.

Being a fan can be an odd choice. I've wondered for a long time about baseball and how it fits in my life. It's about the only thing I've kept from Cascade, certainly the only thing whose stature has not diminished but grown in me in the years since. Bart Giamatti, the Yale classics professor who inexplicably became commissioner of baseball, once wrote that sport and its pursuit of perfection had become a sort of secular religion: "In the main, I agree with the argument that sports can be viewed as a kind of popular or debased religion, in the sense that the most intense feelings are brought to bear or in the sense that sports may mirror whatever avowedly 'sacred' concerns Americans do share. . . . The gods have fled, I know. My

---

* Casey, you're not alone. One of the dozens of teams I have played with had a really bad first baseman who could not handle my throws from shortstop. For some reason, my teammates faulted me. They had a mock uniform shirt made up as a gift for me. On it, where a player's name would ordinarily be, they had written "E-6."

sense is the gods have always been essentially absent. . . . I
believe we have played games, and watched games, to imi-
tate the gods, to become godlike in our worship of each
other and, through those moments of transmutation, to
know for an instant what the gods know."[11]

Well, yes and no. For me, it is not just the gods who
are long gone. Absences abound. It is sometimes easier to
count the things that are present than the things that have
left. I'm not alone in this, I think. We are, all of us, trying
to find what we have lost. Some of us hold on to most of
what we have, dropping just bits and pieces. Others shed
whole skins and several layers beneath. For me, a central
part of what I miss has always been the sense of commu-
nity we had in our hometown. Baseball was inseparable
from that.

At Legion Field, on wet, hot August nights in the late
innings of late-night doubleheaders, when the Reds faced
the Dyersville Hawks, the smoke from the old men's cigars
would roll up toward the glittered sky, mixing with the
steam rising from the old women's cardboard coffee cups,
and float up above the light poles, where the bugs gathered
in their billions. The smoke and the steam and the bugs
obscured the rest of the world, which was just as well; the
rest of the world would have had a hard time competing.
Yet I fled this refuge at the earliest opportunity. And to
a destination—the military—to which I was profoundly
unsuited. What was I running from?

I enjoyed—no, relished—the anonymity of big city
life when I discovered it as an adult. It isn't only baseball pitchers who deceive, and deception isn't something
we do solely, or even mostly, to others. We deceive our-

selves when we think leaving things behind has no cost. It took me years to realize what I had given up in exchange. Belief, belonging, humility, and family were among the things I lost; I have yet to recover any of them completely. Yet baseball remains and provides a faint trail back to that past while my life tumbles on. Baseball offers an invitation, of a sort, to return.

One thing about games—baseball, but others, too—at least for me, is that playing them insinuates them into your psyche. I haven't played basketball seriously since 1995, but I still dream about it almost every night. I gave up playing baseball in 1977, softball in 1992. Certain routine physical movements—getting lined up behind a fly ball, coming across the bag on a double play, the throw from the hole—occur to me at odd moments. I can still see the tailing fastball I threw that broke Pat Callahan's helmet in 1966. In games, you are for once truly outside yourself and yet forcefully present at all times. It must be the sensuousness of the remembered motion that compels the memories. I think we remember the movements as a way to forget what we're missing and celebrate the parts that, if we are lucky, we still have.

Our culture today prizes acceleration, explosion, flash. Baseball at its best is a game played by craftsmen— craftsmen of a very high level, yes, but craftsmen. The game is a grind. You do not persist with flash. That's the secret beauty of baseball. It's not made from some magic dust sprinkled over a cornfield. It's a construction, something built over a very long time. It's made by hand.

We valued that sort of modest beginning where I'm from. Spend enough time in rural Dubuque County and the number of people missing small body parts or functions begins to seem almost usual. Hay balers and combines are cranky machines, and cows can be mean and uncooperative. Let's not even talk about hogs. In my own family, one of my grandfathers, while clearing a field of stumps, lost his sight to a dynamite charge that took too long to reveal itself; a cousin lost a hand to a baler—a machine that scoops up new-mown hay and straw and packages it into twine-wrapped cubes. They're doubtless much more efficient machines now than they were then, but in the years when I worked in the fields, these machines constantly jammed and broke, and somebody was forever sticking his hand in where it shouldn't have been stuck. Mangled digits and lost appendages were a cost of doing business.

Of course, you lose things in the city, too. Youth, sobriety, innocence, honor, love—the list is long, and the absence, though not always apparent, aches like a farmhand's phantom limb. I grieve, as we all do, for the things that are missing. I think about how we treasured what we had in that crowded little Cascade house. With so many in so small a space, the one thing we had more than enough of was people. Maybe that was sufficient, or ought to have been.

Visitors to the Midwest often describe the region as a giant flat plain where the fields form checkerboards, rigid squares proceeding mile after mile with martial precision. The patchwork of fields in eastern Iowa isn't that. Instead, it is a crazy quilt of rectangles, triangles, circles, oblongs, long swooping curves, and blobs—almost every shape there is but a square, all of the shapes following the land's soft swells, bound by limestone gravel roads, small crooked rivers, and ancient stands of maple, hickory, black walnut, and oak that somehow escaped the mill's blades. It's gorgeous country, and I don't get back as much as I should.

When I do, people ask:

"Which one are you?"

Mac's boy, I say, the oldest.

"Umm. Yeah. Want a beer?"

I left town in 1968, and Mac left us all for good eighteen years later. Still, identifying my father was all the information anyone here needs to file me in the proper folder.

"And where are you now?" they ask, as if I had been a particularly hard one to keep track of.

This turns out to be an excellent question. I think the right answer is that I, like us all, have for a very long time been trying to find my way back home.

APPENDIX

The Box Score

Tampa Bay Rays

HITTERS	AB	R	H	RBI	BB	SO			
S Fuld LF	3	0	0	0	0	0			
B Upton CF	3	0	0	0	0	1			
M Joyce RF	3	0	0	0	0	1			
E Longoria DH	3	0	0	0	0	2			
B Zobrist 2B	3	0	0	0	0	1			
C Pena 1B	3	0	0	0	0	1			
J Lobaton C	2	0	0	0	0	1			
a-D Jennings PH	1	0	0	0	0	1			
E Johnson SS	2	0	0	0	0	2			
b-J Keppinger PH	1	0	0	0	0	0			
S Rodriguez 3B	3	0	0	0	0	2			
TOTALS	27	0	0	0	0	12			

a-struck out swinging for J Lobaton in the 9th
b-grounded to shortstop for E Johnson in the 9th

BATTING
Team LOB: 0
FIELDING
E: E Johnson (10, ground ball)
DP: 1 (B Zobrist-C Pena)

Tampa Bay Rays

PITCHERS	IP	H	R	ER	BB	SO	HR	PC-ST	ERA
J Hellickson									
(L, 7-8)	7.0	5	1	1	1	1	0	115-73	3.39
K Farnsworth	1.0	0	0	0	0	1	0	15-9	3.95
TOTALS	8.0	5	1	1	1	2	0	130-82	

PITCHING
WP: J Hellickson
First-pitch strikes/Batters faced: J Hellickson 14/27; K Farnsworth 1/3
Called strikes-Swinging strikes-Foul balls-In Play strikes: J Hellickson 15-11-22-25; K Farnsworth 2-2-3-2
Ground Balls-Fly Balls: J Hellickson 9-10; K Farnsworth 0-2
Game Scores: J Hellickson 63

Seattle Mariners

HITTERS	AB	R	H	RBI	BB	SO			
D Ackley 2B	4	0	1	0	0	0			
M Saunders CF	4	0	0	0	0	0			
J Montero DH	4	0	1	1	0	1			
J Jaso C	3	0	1	0	0	0			
K Seager 3B	3	0	0	0	0	0			
J Smoak 1B	3	0	0	0	0	1			
T Robinson LF	3	0	1	0	0	0			
E Thames RF	2	0	0	0	1	0			
B Ryan SS	3	1	1	0	0	0			
TOTALS	29	1	5	1	1	2			

BATTING
2B: J Jaso (14, J Hellickson)
RBI: J Montero (46)
2-out RBI: J Montero
Mariners RISP: 1-3 (K Seager 0-1, E Thames 0-1, J Montero 1-1)
Team LOB: 5
BASERUNNING
SB: B Ryan (9, 2nd base off J Hellickson/J Lobaton)

Seattle Mariners

PITCHERS	IP	H	R	ER	BB	SO	HR	PC-ST	ERA
F Hernandez									
(W, 11-5)	9.0	0	0	0	0	12	0	113-77	2.60
TOTALS	9.0	0	0	0	0	12	0	113-77	

PITCHING
First-pitch strikes/Batters faced: F Hernandez 16/27
Called strikes-Swinging strikes-Foul balls-In Play strikes: F Hernandez 18-26-18-15
Ground Balls-Fly Balls: F Hernandez 8-7
Game Scores: F Hernandez 99

ACKNOWLEDGMENTS

Thanks to all the ballplayers who talked to me about what they do. Thanks to all the watchers and writers who produce such wondrous stuff in the ever-growing universe of baseball analysis. This world is ridiculously large and luminous, but some of the earliest outposts within it are still among the best: FanGraphs, Baseball-Reference, and BrooksBaseball among them.

Thanks to Lokesh Dhakar for the graphic designs that head each chapter in the book. Thanks to Larry Swanson for helping adapt them.

Thanks to Edward Kastenmeier and his team at Pantheon for their endurance and insight. They include Stella Tan, Andrew Weber, and copy editor extraordinaire Anne Zaroff-Evans, who I am quite certain will add a hyphen to this sentence.

Thanks again to Paul Bresnick for his counsel and support.

Portions of the personal recollections included in the book were originally published in much different form in *The Seattle Times* and the *Los Angeles Times*. Thanks to Kathy Andrisevic, Kathy Triesch, and Rick Zahler in Seattle, and to Roxane Arnold and Roger Smith in Los Angeles.

Foremost, of course, thanks to my family for their endless patience.

NOTES

PREFACE

1. James Shields, *September Nights* (Thomaston, Maine: Cadent Publishing, 2011), p. 62.

1. THE FASTBALL

1. http://sportsillustrated.cnn.com/2012/baseball/mlb/08/17/felix-hernandez-todd-dybas-perfect-game/index.html.
2. Hitters lose about another foot because, in order to hit the ball with maximum efficiency, they actually have to hit it in front of home plate—that is, before it gets there. See, for example, http://www.baseballamerica.com/today/majors/news/2013/2614830.html.
3. Recent analyses have illustrated consistent and large variance of the zone according to who is pitching, who is hitting, who is catching, the count in which the pitch was thrown, and who is umpiring. See, for example, Matthew Carruth's work here: http://www.fangraphs.com/blogs/the-size-of-the-strike-zone-by-count/.
4. Perry Husband, *Downright Filthy Pitching Book 1— The Science of Effective Velocity,* Downright Filthy Pitching Series (Kindle, July 23, 2013), Kindle locations 293–95.
5. Roger Kahn provides one of the most cogent accounts of the evolution of pitching in the game's early years in *The Head Game: Baseball Seen from the Pitcher's Mound* (New York: Harcourt, 2000), pp. 43–73.

6. Author interview with Jeff Smulyan, August 1991. The original article describing the mess can be found at http://community .seattletimes.nwsource.com/archive/?date=19910823&slug =1301434.

7. Author interview with Carl Willis, July 2012.

8. Author interview with John Jaso, November 2012.

9. An All-Star with the Boston Red Sox for many years.

10. A slugging first baseman then with the Detroit Tigers, then the Texas Rangers and now retired due to injuries.

11. Author interview with John Jaso, November 2012.

12. Ibid.

13. The interview conducted by Mariner broadcaster Rick Rizzs is included in *King of Perfection,* a DVD the Mariners produced later.

14. John Thorn, *Baseball in the Garden of Eden: The Secret History of the Early Game* (New York: Simon & Schuster, 2011), p. 122.

15. Ibid., pp. 30–54. The men were Daniel Lucius Adams, William Rufus Wheaton, and Louis Fenn Wadsworth. Later, a set of rules written by Adams in 1857 was discovered, and were authenticated as the first formal set of rules for the game, elevating his claim as the true inventor.

16. John J. Evers and Hugh S. Fullterton, *Touching Second: The Science of Baseball* (Chicago: Reilly & Britton, 1910), Kindle locations 1241–43.

17. Martin Quigley, *The Crooked Pitch: An Account of the Curveball in American Baseball History* (Chapel Hill, N.C.: Algonquin Books, 1984), p. 72. This is a charming book stuffed with anecdote. Though it's out of print, it's worth tracking down a copy.

18. Feller pitched for the Cleveland Indians in the 1930s through the early '50s, Grove for Philadelphia and Boston in the 1920s and '30s, Gibson for the Cardinals in the 1960s and '70s, Ryan for four teams in a remarkable twenty-seven-year career ending in 1993, and Clemens for four teams for twenty-four years ending in 2007.

19. http://www.ussmariner.com/2007/06/27/an-open-letter-to -rafael-chaves/.

20. Since 1923, to be precise, according to Bill James and Rob Neyer's encyclopedic history, *The Neyer/James Guide to Pitchers: An Historical Compendium of Pitching, Pitchers, and Pitches* (New York: Simon & Schuster/Fireside, 2004), p. 6. This book, the single best source for information about pitching and its evolution, is astonishing in its erudition and especially scope.

21. http://www.fangraphs.com/blogs/qa-felix-hernandez/.

22. He's changed teams several times since but has always struggled for playing time.

23. Author interview with Sam Fuld, December 2012.

24. Ibid.

25. It's worth noting that Hernandez is typical of Major League pitchers, most of whom are much more apt to throw fastballs early in the count or when they are behind in it, and more likely to throw off-speed pitches when they are ahead. See, for example, http://www.fangraphs.com/blogs/the-most-backward-starters-in-mlb/.

26. Adair, Robert K. *The Physics of Baseball: Third Edition, Revised, Updated, and Expanded* (New York: HarperCollins, 2002). Kindle edition (2015), location 1488.

27. Author interview with Sam Fuld.

28. Ibid.

2. THE CURVEBALL

1. Martin Quigley, *The Crooked Pitch: An Account of the Curveball in American Baseball History* (Chapel Hill, N.C.: Algonquin Books, 1984), pp. 37–40.

2. These descriptions are related in ibid., but originated in an interview Cummings gave to *The Sporting News* in 1921, years after his retirement.

3. The early history of pitching is covered in some detail in Roger Kahn, *The Head Game: Baseball Seen from the Pitcher's Mound* (New York: Harcourt, 2000); Quigley, *Crooked Pitch;* and John Thorn, *Baseball in the Garden of Eden: The Secret History of the Early Game* (New York: Simon & Schuster, 2011). The best and by far most entertaining overview is

"What Do You Call That Thing?," the opening essay in Bill James and Rob Neyer, *The Neyer/James Guide to Pitchers: An Historical Compendium of Pitching, Pitchers, and Pitches* (New York: Simon & Schuster/Fireside, 2004).

4. http://www.sptimes.com/2005/05/17/Sports/Here_s_the_pitch.shtml.

5. Jane Leavy, *Koufax: A Lefty's Legacy* (New York: Harper-Collins, 2002), p. 140.

6. Ibid., p. 136.

7. Bill James has written that Wells's curveball differed from most through his exceptional control of it. He "had the best 12-to-6 curve ball that I ever saw. Koufax's curve was thrown hard; Wells not so hard, but Wells had phenomenal control of it. He was able to drop the curve at the very bottom of the strike zone, falling at a tremendous angle, pitch after pitch after pitch." (BJOL http://www.billjamesonline.com/hey_bill/#40297.)

8. These numbers are from the Web site FanGraphs—www.fangraphs.com—which is one of several astonishingly thorough sites providing an ever more detailed and complex variety of data and analysis on major league baseball. Baseball-Reference (www.baseball-reference.com) and BrooksBaseball (www.brooksbaseball.net) are two of the other more innovative sites. Much of the work on these sites was initially done by amateurs, and much was unpaid, although that has changed. The amount of collective effort, both professional and amateur, that goes into the enterprise of analyzing baseball is remarkable.

9. These data come from www.baseball-reference.com, whose sortable statistics include data from every game played since 1916.

10. James Shields, *September Nights* (Thomaston, Maine: Cadent Publishing, 2011), p. 63.

11. Morgan Ensberg, a Houston Astro third baseman in the 2000s, summarized the case against guessing when asked how he thought it hurt his performance: "Guess hitting was bad for me because I never guessed correctly," he said (http://

www.hardballtimes.com/nuts-and-bolts-of-hitting-in-the-big
-leagues-with-morgan-ensberg/).

3. THE SPITBALL

1. Brian Cooper, *Red Faber: A Biography of the Hall of Famer Spitball Pitcher* (Jefferson, N.C.: McFarland and Company, 2007), p. 28. This recent full-length biography of Faber is the only one that exists, and almost all of the biographical details in my account are drawn from it.
2. http://www.billjamesonline.com/hey_bill/.
3. Cooper, *Red Faber*, p. 29.
4. *Baseball Magazine*, September 1922.
5. Ruth was regarded as a new style of hitter, one who swung freely and for the fences. As William F. McNeil points out in his excellent history, *The Evolution of Pitching in Major League Baseball* (Jefferson, N.C.: McFarland and Company, 2006), free swinging has been taken to an entirely different level in today's game. Ruth hit for high averages and struck out on average just eighty-seven times a year. "In today's game, Ruth would be considered a contact hitter," McNeil writes.
6. http://sabr.org/bioproj/person/d9fdc289.

4. THE SINKER

1. http://news.berkeley.edu/2013/05/08/motion-vision/. Maus and colleagues at the University of California, Berkeley, have determined that the brain estimates a moving object's trajectory extremely accurately from information gathered in the first milliseconds of observed flight. Otherwise, you would never have a chance of hitting a ball thrown at big league speed. A pitched ball would be by you almost before you saw it. A hitter's brain makes a prediction as to where the pitch will be when it reaches him. Ted Williams, the great Boston Red Sox hitter—perhaps the greatest hitter for any team ever—famously said that he could see the pitched ball hit the bat. No, he almost certainly could not, but he was excellent at pre-

dicting where the ball would hit the bat. For more on Maus's work, see here: http://www.quantumday.com/2013/05/v5 -region-of-visual-cortex-responsible.html. In fact, not only couldn't Williams see the ball hit the bat; he, like almost all hitters, lost sight of the ball entirely at some point during its transit. See description of the process here: https://www .baseballprospectus.com/article.php?articleid=17405.

2. Robert K. Adair, *The Physics of Baseball: Third Edition, Revised, Updated, and Expanded* (New York: HarperCollins, 2002), pp. 50–51. Kindle edition (2015), locations 840–42.

3. Ibid., p. 51. Adair, Robert K. *The Physics of Baseball.* Kindle location 842.

4. Maddux knew intuitively what research would later authenticate—hitters are much more likely to swing on 3-2 than 2-2. They swing at balls in and out of the zone at higher rates, according to game theorist Matt Swartz. See http:// www.hardballtimes.com/game-theory-is-the-next-moneyball /#When:06:06:15.

5. This originally appeared on a Boston Red Sox fan site in 2004, but the archives appear to have been scrubbed. The home page for the site, *The Sons of Sam Horn,* is here: http:// sonsofsamhorn.net/.

6. *Seattle Times,* Aug. 10, 2005, accessed at http://seattletimes .com/html/sports/2002430892_mari10.html.

7. http://www.fangraphs.com/blogs/index.php/qa-felix-hernan dez/. This is one of an extensive, insightful series of interviews with pitchers conducted by David Laurila. The series started when he worked for Baseball Prospectus and continues now at FanGraphs. The interviews are fascinating throughout.

8. http://brooksbaseball.net/tabs.php?player=433587&gFilt= &time=game&minmax=ci&var=ra&s_type=2&startDate= 01/01/2012&endDate=08/14/2012.

9. Another excellent Laurila interview: http://www.fangraphs .com/blogs/index.php/qa-bob-mcclure-on-banny-simba -deception/.

10. Perry Husband, *Downright Filthy Pitching Book 1—The Science of Effective Velocity,* Downright Filthy Pitching Series (Kindle, July 23, 2013), locations 309–11.

11. http://baseballanalysts.com/archives/2009/03/home_run _rate_b.php.

12. Author interview with Carl Willis, July 2012.

13. http://www.fangraphs.com/blogs/index.php/qa-bob-mcclure -on-banny-simba-deception/.

14. Willis interview.

15. http://www.brooksbaseball.net/profile.php?player=433587 &balls=-1&strikes=-1&b_hand=-1&time=month&minmax =ci&var=count&s_type=2&gFilt=&pFilt=FA|SI|FC|CU|SL |CS|KN|CH|FS|SB&startDate=&endDate=.

16. Hernandez's curve has since continued to improve, and in recent years he has had an average spin rate of more than two thousand. All of these data are generated by the MLB-installed pitch f/x system of digital cameras and analysis. The numbers I am using come from the Web site BrooksBaseball, which has a frankly astonishing amount of information. See, for example, the pitch data for Hernandez during this game at http://www.brooksbaseball.net/pfxVB/tabdel_expanded.php ?pitchSel=433587&game=gid_2012_08_15_tbamlb_seamlb _1/&s_type=&h_size=700&v_size=500.

17. http://www.baseballprospectus.com/article. php?articleid=22156.

18. Author interview with Sam Fuld.

19. Mariner's DVD *King of Perfection.*

20. McCracken's story has been told expertly many times. An excellent summary of his career by Jeff Passan can be found here: http://www.thepostgame.com/features/201101 /sabermetrician-exile.

21. http://www.baseballprospectus.com/article.php?articleid=878.

5. THE KNUCKLEBALL

1. Christy Mathewson, *Pitching in a Pinch: Or, Baseball from the Inside,* Every Boy's Library (New York: Grosset & Dunlap, 1912), p. 11.

2. Robert K. Adair, *The Physics of Baseball: Third Edition, Revised, Updated, and Expanded* (New York: HarperCollins, 2002), p. 54. Kindle edition (2015), locations 894–95.

3. Robert Watts and Eric Sawyer, "Aerodynamics of a Knuckleball," *American Journal of Physics,* Nov. 1975, p. 9, accessed at http://baseball.physics.illinois.edu/WattsSawyerAJP.pdf.
4. Jim Bouton, *Ball Four,* (RosettaBooks Sports Classics), Kindle edition, location 566.
5. Bouton quoted in Ben McGrath, "Project Knuckleball," *New Yorker,* May 17, 2004, accessed at http://www.newyorker.com/magazine/2004/05/17/project-knuckleball.
6. R. A. Dickey, *Wherever I End Up: My Quest for Truth, Authenticity, and the Perfect Knuckleball* (New York: Blue Rider Press, 2012), p. 150.
7. Author interview with Carl Willis, August 2012.
8. Mariners DVD, *King of Perfection.*
9. Author interview with John Jaso.

6. THE SLIDER

1. Mariners DVD, *King of Perfection.*
2. http://www.fangraphs.com/blogs/qa-bronson-arroyo-master-craftsman/.
3. Author interview with Elliot Johnson, January 2013.
4. Author interview with Carl Willis.
5. *Ball Four,* Kindle Location 1244.
6. E-mail interview with Ron Fairly, December 2012. Fairly was the Dodgers' first baseman at the time and said he was told the story by Roseboro.
7. Tim McCarver, *Baseball for Brain Surgeons and Other Fans* (New York: Villard, 1998), p. 50.
8. Bill James and Rob Neyer, *The Neyer/James Guide to Pitchers: An Historical Compendium of Pitching, Pitchers, and Pitches* (New York: Simon & Schuster/Fireside, 2004), p. 157.

7. THE SPLIT

1. Bill James and Rob Neyer, *The Neyer/James Guide to Pitchers: An Historical Compendium of Pitching, Pitchers, and Pitches* (New York: Simon & Schuster/Fireside, 2004), p. 18. You really should buy this book.

2. Ibid.

3. "Split-Finger Fastball, Once Popular, Is Falling Away," *New York Times,* Oct. 1, 2011, accessed at http://www.nytimes.com/2011/10/02/sports/baseball/split-finger-fastball-use-of-a-popular-pitch-falls-off-the-table.html?_r=0.

4. http://blogs.seattletimes.com/hotstoneleague/2012/08/16/rays_manager_joe_maddon_denies/.

5. Author interview with Sam Fuld.

6. Ibid.

7. http://www.fangraphs.com/blogs/john-dewan-jeter-vs-ryan-and-10x10-buckets/.

8. http://www.baseballprospectus.com/article.php?articleid=12965.

9. http://sabr.org/latest/carruth-size-strike-zone-count.

10. Mariners DVD, *King of Perfection.*

11. Ibid.

8. THE CUTTER

1. Author interview with John Jaso.

9. THE CHANGE

1. Author interview with Elliot Johnson.

2. Author interview with John Jaso.

3. Mariners DVD, *King of Perfection.*

4. Ibid.

5. Ibid.

6. Ibid.

7. Ibid.

8. Ibid.

9. Author interview with Carl Willis.

10. Author interview with John Jaso.

11. A. Bartlett Giamatti, *Take Time for Paradise: Americans and Their Games* (New York: Summit Books, 1989), pp. 13, 24–25.

A NOTE ABOUT THE AUTHOR

Terry McDermott is a former national reporter for the *Los Angeles Times* and the author of three previous books: *The Hunt for KSM: Inside the Pursuit and Takedown of the Real 9/11 Mastermind, Khalid Sheikh Mohammed* (co-authored with Josh Meyer); *101 Theory Drive: The Discovery of Memory;* and *Perfect Soldiers: The 9/11 Hijackers—Who They Were, Why They Did It.*